Colour Plate 1.   Rembrandt van Rijn, The Artist in his Studio, c.1629, oil on panel, 24.8 x 31.7 cm. Museum of Fine Arts, Boston, Zoë Oliver Sherman Collection, given in memory of Lillie Oliver Poor (38.1838). (Courtesy of The Museum of Fine Arts, Boston.)

W9-ARR-571

Colour Plate 2. Frederick Church, Twilight in the Wilderness, 1860, oil on canvas, 101.6 x 162.6 cm. Cleveland Museum of Art, Mr and Mrs William H. Marlatt Fund (1965.233).
(© 1997 The Cleveland Museum of Art.)

Colour Plate 3.   John Russell, The Face of the Moon, c.1795, pastel on paper, 64.14 x 46.99 cm. City Museum and Art Gallery, Birmingham. (Photograph: courtesy of The Birmingham Museums and Art Gallery.)

Colour Plate 4. Giovanni di Paolo, St John the Baptist going into the Wilderness, c.1450, tempera on panel, 31 x 38 cm. National Gallery, London. (Reproduced by courtesy of the Trustees, The National Gallery, London.)

Colour Plate 5. Piero della Francesca, The Flagellation of Christ, c.1460, tempera on panel, 58 x 81 cm. National Gallery of the Marches, Ducal Palace, Urbino. (Photograph: Scala.)

Colour Plate 6.   Claude Monet, Ice Floes (formerly titled The Thaw), 1893, oil on canvas, 66 x 100.3 cm. Metropolitan Museum of Art, New York, H.O. Havemeyer Collection, bequest of Mrs H.O. Havemeyer, 1929 (29.100.108).

Colour Plate 7.   Joseph Wright of Derby, The Earth-stopper on the Banks of the Derwent, 1773, oil on canvas, 96 x 121 cm. Derby Museums and Art Gallery.

Colour Plate 8. Louise Moillon, Still Life (with a Basket of Fruit and a Bunch of Asparagus), c. 1630, oil on cradled panel, 53.3 x 71.3 cm. Art Institute of Chicago, Wirt D. Walker Fund (1948.78). (Photograph: © 1996 The Art Institute of Chicago. All rights reserved.)

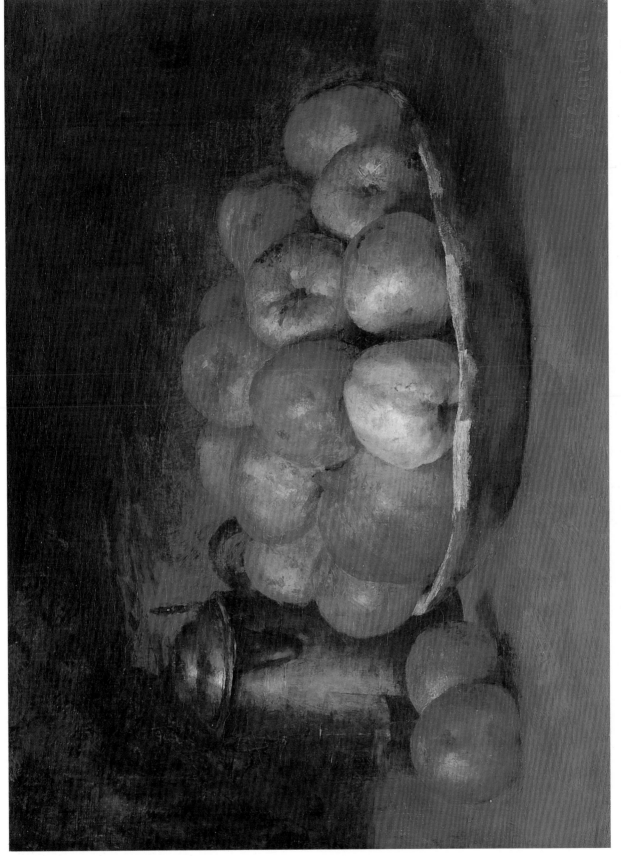

Colour Plate 9. Gustave Courbet, Still Life with Apples and Pomegranate, 1876, oil on canvas, 44.5 x 61 cm. National Gallery, London. (Reproduced by courtesy of the Trustees, The National Gallery, London.)

Colour Plate 10. Harmen Steenwyck, Still Life: An Allegory of the Vanities of Human Life, 1621, oil on oak panel, 39.2 x 50.7 cm. National Gallery, London. (Reproduced by courtesy of the Trustees, The National Gallery, London.)

Colour Plate 11.   Jan Davidsz de Heem, Still Life with Fruit and Oysters, 1643, oil on panel, 65 x 87 cm. Ashmolean Museum, Oxford.

Colour Plate 12.   Claude Monet, Lavacourt, 1880, oil on canvas, 98 x 149 cm. Dallas Museum of Art, Munger Fund.

Colour Plate 13. Jackson Pollock, Summertime Number 9A, 1948, oil, enamel and housepaint on canvas, 85 x 550 cm. Tate Gallery, London. (© 1998 ARS, New York and DACS, London.)

Colour Plate 14. Sestertius of Titus, c. 80 CE, bronze, 1.5 cm diameter. British Museum, London. (Reproduced by permission of the Trustees of the British Museum.)

Colour Plate 15. Colosseum, Rome, 70–80 CE, view across present-day arena. (Photograph: Scala.)

Colour Plate 16. *Hunt of wild animals, third century* CE, *mosaic, from House of Bacchus, Cuicul, Algeria. Djemila Museum, Algeria. (Reproduced from R. Luciani, Il Colosseo, Milan, Istituto Geografico De Agostini Novara, 1990, p.150; photograph: G. Dagli Orti.)*

Colour Plate 17. 'Magerius', third century CE, mosaic, 440 × 220 cm, from Smirat, Tunisia. Sousse Museum, Tunisia. (Photograph: Ancient Art and Architecture Collection.)

Colour Plate 18. Amphitheatre at Pompeii, 59 CE, fresco. Naples Museum. (Photograph: Scala.)

Colour Plate 19. (Main picture) Colosseum, Rome, aerial view. (Photograph: Index/Fotografia Vasari, Rome.)

Colour Plate 20. (Inset) Fry, Drew, Knight & Creamer, Arts Faculty building, The Open University, 1969–70. (Photograph: Mike Levers/The Open University.)

Colour Plate 21. Pantheon, Rome, 118–c. 128 CE, section, 52.6 x 74.5 cm. Sir John Soane's Museum, London (45/3/53). (Reproduced by courtesy of the Trustees of Sir John Soane's Museum.)

Colour Plate 22.   Arch of Constantine, Rome, 315 CE. (Photograph: Colin Cunningham.)

Colour Plate 23.   Santa Maria Novella, Florence, 1456–70, façade by Leon Battista Alberti.
(Photograph: Scala.)

Colour Plate 24. John Wood, King's Circus, Bath, 1740 onwards. (Photograph: A.F. Kersting.)

Colour Plate 25.   James Scott, Elphinstone Circle (later Horniman Circle), Bombay, 1864 onwards. (Photograph: Colin Cunningham.)

Colour Plate 26.   Colosseum, Rome, view of interior. (Photograph: Colin Cunningham.)

Colour Plate 27.   Colosseum, Rome, detail of restored seating. (Photograph: Colin Cunningham.)

Colour Plate 28. Colosseum, Rome, detail of Ionic arcade. (Photograph: Index/Fotografia Vasari, Rome.)

Colour Plate 29. Colosseum, Rome, inner arcades and bases of vaults. (Photograph: Colin Cunningham.)

Colour Plate 30. Sir John Soane, section of the Colosseum with the King's Circus in Bath drawn to scale inside it, 5 November 1814, ink and watercolour on paper, 60.2 × 122 cm. Sir John Soane's Museum, London (23/2/1). (Reproduced by courtesy of the Trustees of Sir John Soane's Museum.)

Colour Plate 31. Trajan's Forum, Rome, 100–122 CE. (Photograph: Colin Cunningham.)

Colour Plate 32. Palace of Porphyrogenitus (Turkish modern name Tekfur Sarayi), Istanbul, early fourteenth century. (Photograph: Werner Foreman Archive.)

Colour Plate 33. Filippo Brunelleschi, Pazzi Chapel, Santa Croce, Florence, 1429–61. (Photograph: Scala.)

Colour Plate 34. Filippo Brunelleschi, Ospedale degli Innocenti, Florence, 1419 onwards, loggia. (Photograph: Scala.)

Colour Plate 35. K.I. Rossi, General Staff Headquarters, St Petersburg, Russia, 1819–25. (Photograph: Colin Cunningham.)

Colour Plate 36. Chelsea Football Ground, London, 1990, east stand. (Photograph: Mike Levers/The Open University.)

Colour Plate 37. Pierre-Auguste Renoir, Path Climbing through the Long Grass, 1876–7, oil on canvas, 60 x 74 cm. Musée d'Orsay, Paris. (Photograph: © Réunion des Musées Nationaux – C. Jean.)

Colour Plate 38. François Boucher, Diana Leaving her Bath, 1742, oil on canvas, 56 x 73 cm. Musée du Louvre, Paris. (Photograph: © Réunion des Musées Nationaux – Hervé Lewandowski.)

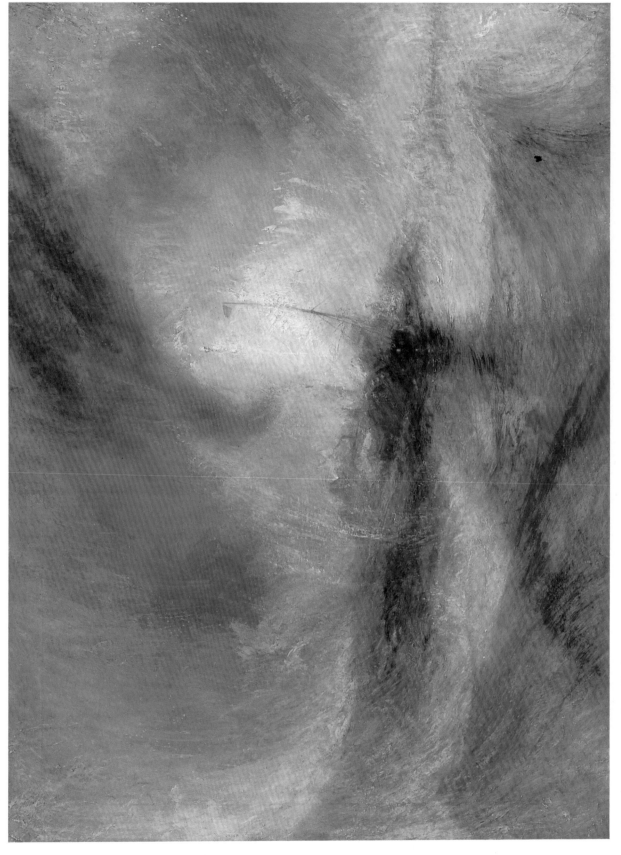

Colour Plate 39. Joseph Mallord William Turner, Snowstorm: Steamboat off a Harbour's Mouth, 1842, oil on canvas, 91.4 x 12.19 cm. Tate Gallery, London. (Photograph: John Webb.)

Colour Plate 40.   Pablo Picasso, Girl in a Chemise, *c.1905, oil on canvas, 72.7 x 60 cm. Tate Gallery, London.*
(© 1998 Succession Picasso, DACS, London.)

Colour Plate 41. Jacques-Louis David, The Lictors Returning to Brutus the Bodies of his Sons, 1789, oil on canvas, 325 x 422 cm. Musée du Louvre, Paris. (Photograph: © Réunion des Musées Nationaux – G. Biot/C. Jean.)

Colour Plate 42. Jacques-Louis David, The Loves of Paris and Helen, 1788–89, oil on canvas, 146 x 181 cm. Musée du Louvre, Paris. (Photograph: © Réunion des Musées Nationaux – C. Jean.)

Colour Plate 43. Jacques-Louis David, The Oath of the Horatii, 1785, oil on canvas, 330 x 425 cm. Musée du Louvre, Paris. (Photograph: © Réunion des Musées Nationaux – G. Biot/C. Jean.)

Colour Plate 44. Jacques-Louis David, The Death of Socrates, 1787, oil on canvas, 129.5 x 196.2 cm. Metropolitan Museum of Art, New York, Catharine Lorillard Wolfe Collection, Wolfe Fund, 1931 (31.45).

Colour Plate 45.   Revolutionary wallpaper symbolizing the 'mountain' surmounted by the 'rights of man' smiting France's enemies, 1794 (?). Private collection. (Photograph: Edimedia, Paris.)

Colour Plate 46.   Jacques-Louis David, The Death of Marat, 1793, oil on canvas, 160 x 125 cm. Musées Royaux des Beaux-Arts de Belgique, Brussels. (© ACL Brussels; photograph: Cussac.)

Colour Plate 47. Jacques-Louis David, Bonaparte Crossing the Alps at Mont Saint Bernard, *1800–1, oil on canvas, 260 x 221 cm. Musée National du Chateau de Malmaison (49.7.1). (Photograph: Lauros–Giraudon.)*

Colour Plate 48. Jacques-Louis David, The Sabine Women, 1799, oil on canvas, 386 x 520 cm. Musée du Louvre, Paris. (Photograph: © Réunion des Musées Nationaux – R.G. Ojeda.)

Colour Plate 49. Nicolas Poussin, The Triumph of Pan, 1635–6, oil on canvas, 134 x 145 cm. National Gallery, London. (Reproduced by courtesy of the Trustees, The National Gallery, London.)

Colour Plate 50.   Raphael, The Alba Madonna, c.1510, oil on panel transferred to canvas, 94.5 cm diameter. National Gallery of Art, Washington, D.C., Andrew W. Mellon Collection. (© 1997 Board of Trustees, The National Gallery of Art, Washington, D.C.)

Colour Plate 51. Rococo interior, showing paintings in context, Germain Boffrand, Hôtel de Soubise, Paris, interior of the Salon de la Princesse, c.1735. (Photograph: Bulloz.)

Colour Plate 52.   Jacques-Louis David, Charlotte David, 1813, oil on canvas, 72.9 x 59.4 cm. National Gallery of Art, Washington, D.C., Samuel H. Kress Collection. (© 1997 Board of Trustees, The National Gallery of Art, Washington, D.C.)

*Colour Plate 53.   Caspar David Friedrich, The Tetschen Altar or Cross in the Mountains, 1808, oil, 115 x 110 cm.
Staatliche Kunstsammlungen, Gemäldegalerie, Dresden.*

Colour Plate 54.   Mathis Grünewald, Angels' Concert *(left) and* The Nativity *(right), 1515, panels of the Isenheim altarpiece, oil on panel, 269 x 142, 265 x 152 cm. Musée d'Unterlinden, Colmar. (Photograph: Giraudon.)*

Colour Plate 55.   Claude Lorraine, Landscape with Hagar and the Angel, 1646, oil on canvas, 52 x 44 cm. National Gallery, London. (Reproduced by courtesy of the Trustees, The National Gallery, London.)

Colour Plate 56.   Jean-Baptiste Regnault, Descent from the Cross, 1789, oil on canvas, 425 x
233 cm. Musée du Louvre, Paris. (Photograph: © Réunion des Musées Nationaux – R.G. Ojeda.)

Colour Plate 57. Caspar David Friedrich, Monk by the Sea, 1809, oil, 110 x 171 cm. Staatliche Museen zu Berlin Preussischer Kulturbesitz Nationalgalerie. (Photograph: Jörg P. Anders.)

Colour Plate 58.   Caspar David Friedrich, Abbey in the Oak Forest, 1809–10, oil on canvas, 110.4 x 171 cm. Staatliche Museen zu Berlin Preussischer Kulturbesitz Nationalgalerie. (Photograph: Jörg P. Anders.)

Colour Plate 59. Caspar David Friedrich, Arctic Shipwreck, 1824, oil, 97 x 127 cm. Kunsthalle, Hamburg. (Photograph: Elke Walford, Hamburg.)

Colour Plate 60. Caspar David Friedrich, Wanderer above the Sea of Fog, c.1818, oil on canvas, 98.4 x 74.8 cm. Kunsthalle, Hamburg. (Photograph: Elke Walford, Hamburg.)

Colour Plate 61. Caspar David Friedrich, Moonrise over the Sea, 1822, oil on canvas, 55 x 71 cm. Staatliche Museen zu Berlin Preussischer Kulturbesitz Nationalgalerie. (Photograph: Jörg P. Anders.)

Colour Plate 62. Caspar David Friedrich, Woman before the Setting Sun, c.1818–20, oil, 22 x 30 cm. Museum Folkwang, Essen.

Colour Plate 63.   Caspar David Friedrich, Two Men Contemplating the Moon, 1819, oil on canvas, 35 x 44 cm. Staatliche Kunstsammlungen, Gemäldegalerie, Dresden.

Colour Plate 64. Caspar David Friedrich, The Chasseur in the Forest, 1813–14, oil on canvas, 65.7 x 46.7 cm. Private collection.

Colour Plate 65.   Caspar David Friedrich, View of Arkona with Rising Moon, 1806, pencil and sepia, 61 x 100 cm. Graphische Sammlung, Albertina, Vienna.

Colour Plate 66. Caspar David Friedrich, The Large Enclosure near Dresden, 1832, oil on canvas, 73.5 × 103 cm. Staatliche Kunstsammlungen, Gemäldegalerie, Dresden.

Colour Plate 67.   Caspar David Friedrich, Winter Landscape with Church, probably 1811, oil on canvas, 32.5 x 45 cm. National Gallery, London. (Reproduced by courtesy of the Trustees, The National Gallery, London.)

Colour Plate 68. Medea, wearing a Phrygian helmet, escapes from Corinth driving a chariot drawn by dragons, Lucanian red-figure calyx krater, c.400 BCE, 51.4 cm high, The Cleveland Museum of Art, Leonard C. Hanna Jr Fund. The vase is earthenware with slip decoration and added red, white and yellow, attributed to the Policoro painter. Jason is shown in a state of helplessness below Medea's chariot. It is Medea who dominates the scene, surrounded by sun rays, emphasizing her relationship to the sun-god Helios (her grandfather, see Medea, line 1321). Medea's two dead sons lie on an altar to the right of the scene, mourned by the nurse and tutor. Two winged Furies observe the scene. Jason cannot act to stop Medea and his position below her reinforces his now inferior status and his defeat. This contrasts with the conventionally 'heroic' depiction of Jason on vases which predate Euripides' play (431 BCE).

Colour Plate 69.   Eugene Delacroix, Medea and her Children, 1838, oil on canvas, 260 x 165 cm, Musée des Beaux Arts, Lille. (Photograph: RMN – P. Bernard.)

Colour Plate 70. John Waterhouse, The Magic Circle, 1886, oil on canvas, 183 x 127 cm, Tate Gallery, London, presented by the Trustees of the Chantrey Bequest, 1886. Waterhouse had a particular interest in female sorcery. Here a woman is shown by a steaming cauldron. She has a snake coiled round her neck and herbs tucked into her dress. These symbolize both witchcraft and healing power. (© The Tate Gallery, London.)

Colour Plate 71.   Mark Rothko, Black on Maroon, 1958, oil on canvas, 266.7 x 365.8 cm. Tate Gallery, London.
(© 1998 ARS, NY and DACS, London.)

Colour Plate 72.   Mark Rothko, Black on Maroon, 1958, oil on canvas, 241.3 x 266.7 cm. Tate Gallery, London.
(© 1998 ARS, NY and DACS, London.)

Colour Plate 73. Mark Rothko, Black on Maroon, *1958, oil on canvas, 228.6 x 207 cm. Tate Gallery, London.*
(© 1998 ARS, NY and DACS, London.)

Colour Plate 74.   Mark Rothko, Black on Maroon, 1959, oil on canvas, 266.7 x 457.2 cm. Tate Gallery, London.
(© 1998 ARS, NY and DACS, London.)

Colour Plate 75. Mark Rothko, Black on Maroon, 1959, oil on canvas, 228.6 x 266.7 cm. Tate Gallery, London. (© 1998 ARS, NY and DACS, London.)

Colour Plate 76.   Mark Rothko, Red on Maroon, 1959, oil on canvas, 266.7 x 238.8 cm. Tate Gallery, London.
(© 1998 ARS, NY and DACS, London.)

Colour Plate 77. Mark Rothko, Red on Maroon, 1959, oil on canvas, 182.9 x 457.2 cm. Tate Gallery, London. (© 1998 ARS, NY and DACS, London.)

Colour Plate 78.   Mark Rothko, Red on Maroon, 1959, oil on canvas, 266.7 x 457.2 cm. Tate Gallery, London.
(© 1998 ARS, NY and DACS, London.)

Colour Plate 79.   Mark Rothko, Red on Maroon, 1959, oil on canvas, 182.9 x 457.2 cm. Tate Gallery, London.
(© 1998 ARS, NY and DACS, London.)

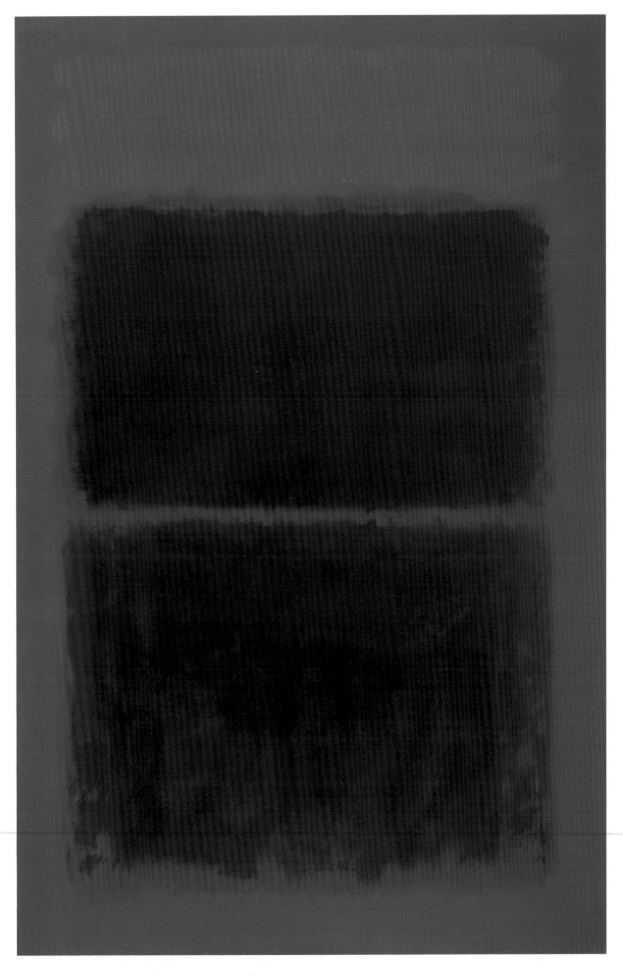

Colour Plate 80. Mark Rothko, Light Red over Black, *1957, oil on canvas, 232.7 x 152.7 cm. Tate Gallery, London. (© 1998 ARS, NY and DACS, London.)*

Colour Plate 81. Andy Warhol, Red Race Riot, 1963, synthetic polymer paint and silkscreen on canvas, 334 x 212 cm, Museum Ludwig, Cologne. (© 1998 ARS, NY and DACS, London.)

Colour Plate 82. Andy Warhol, Sixteen Jackies, 1964, acrylic, enamel and silkscreen on canvas,
16 panels each 50.8 x 40.6 cm, overall 204 x 162 cm, Walker Art Center, Minneapolis, Art Center Acquisition Fund.
(© 1998 ARS, NY and DACS, London.)

Colour Plate 83.   Andy Warhol, Gold Marilyn Monroe, 1962, synthetic polymer paint, silkscreen and oil on canvas, 211 x 145 cm, Museum of Modern Art, New York, gift of Philip Johnson. (© 1998 The Museum of Modern Art, New York and ARS, NY and DACS, London.)

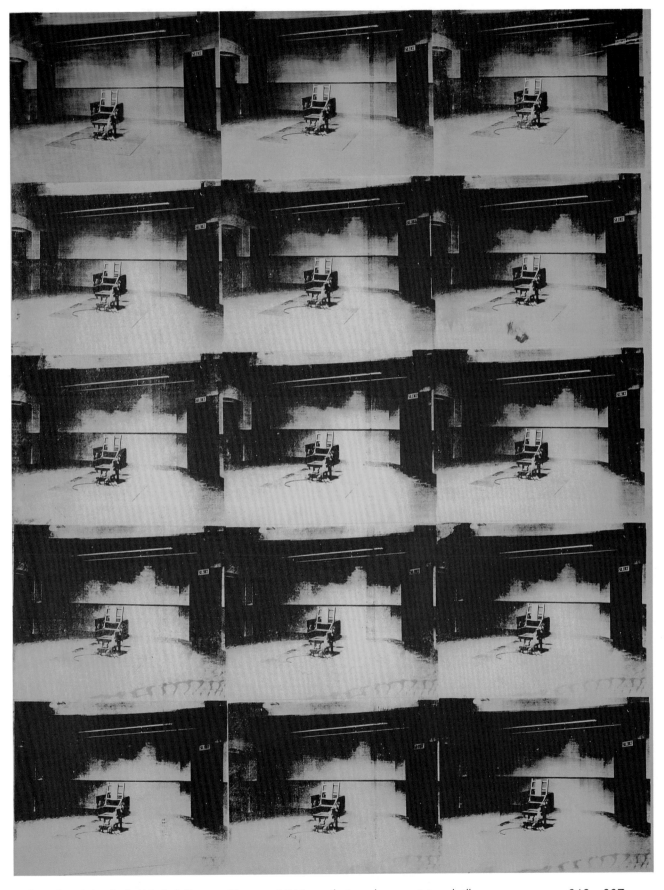

Colour Plate 84. Andy Warhol, Orange Disaster, 1963, synthetic polymer paint and silkscreen on canvas, 269 x 207 cm, gift of the Harry N. Abrams Family Collection. (Photograph: David Heald. © 1998 The Solomon R. Guggenheim Foundation, New York and ARS, NY and DACS, London.)

Colour Plate 85. Mark Rothko, Subway Scene, c.1938, oil on canvas, 89 x 120 cm, Estate of Mark Rothko, Kate Rothko Prizel Collection. (© 1998 ARS, NY and DACS, London.)

Colour Plate 86. Mark Rothko, Slow Swirl by the Edge of the Sea, 1944, oil on canvas, 191 x 215 cm, Museum of Modern Art, New York, bequest of Mrs Mark Rothko through the Mark Rothko Foundation Inc. (© 1998 The Museum of Modern Art, New York and ARS, NY and DACS, London.)

Colour Plate 87.   Mark Rothko, Number 18, c.1947–8, oil on canvas, 155 x 110 cm, National Gallery of Art, Washington, D.C., gift of the Mark Rothko Foundation. (© 1998 Board of Trustees, The National Gallery of Art, Washington D.C. and ARS, NY and DACS, London.)

Colour Plate 88. Mark Rothko, Number 12, 1951, mixed media on canvas, 146 x 138 cm, Estate of Mark Rothko, Christopher Rothko Collection. (© 1998 ARS, NY and DACS, London.)

Colour Plate 89. Mark Rothko, Untitled, 1954, oil on unprimed canvas, 236.3 x 142.7 cm, Yale University Art Gallery, New Haven, Katherine Ordway Collection. (© 1998 ARS, NY and DACS, London.)

Colour Plate 90.
Vincent Van Gogh, The
Night Café, Arles, 1888,
oil on canvas, 70 x 89
cm, Yale University Art
Gallery, New Haven.

Colour Plate 91. Piet Mondrian, Composition in Yellow, Blue and White I, 1937, oil on canvas, 57 x 55 cm, Museum of Modern Art, New York, Sidney and Harriet Janis Collection. (© 1998 The Museum of Modern Art, New York and ARS, NY and DACS, London.)

Colour Plate 92. Le Valentin (Valentin de Boulogne), The Four Ages of Man, 1629–30, oil on canvas, 96.5 x 134 cm, National Gallery, London. (Reproduced by courtesy of the Trustees, The National Gallery, London.)

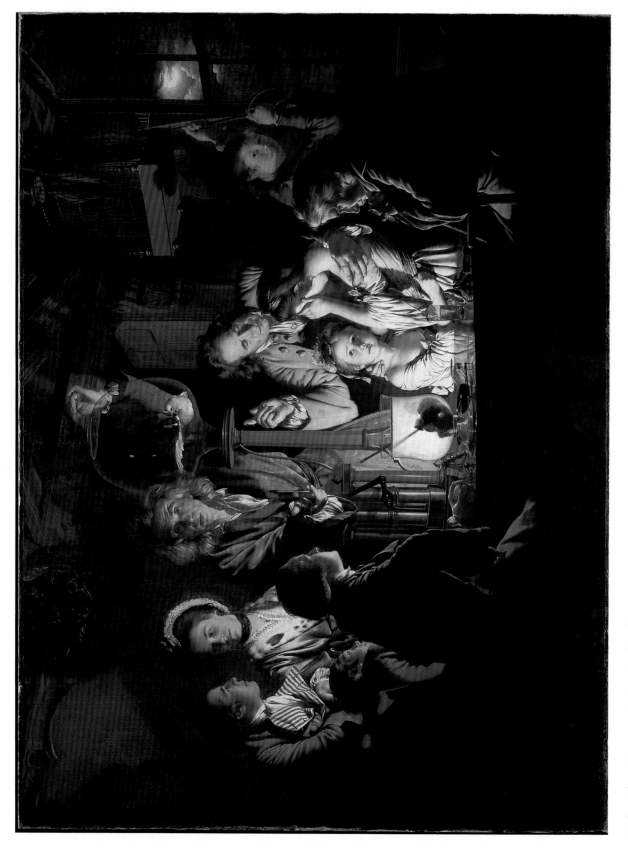

Colour Plate 93. Joseph Wright of Derby, An Experiment on a Bird in the Air Pump, 1768, oil on canvas, 183 x 244 cm, National Gallery, London. (Reproduced by courtesy of the Trustees, The National Gallery, London.)

Colour Plate 94. Elisabeth-Louise Vigée-Lebrun, Self-portrait in a Straw Hat, after 1782, oil on canvas, 98 x 71 cm, National Gallery, London. (Reproduced by courtesy of the Trustees, The National Gallery, London.)

Colour Plate 95. Pierre-Auguste Renoir, The Umbrellas (Les Parapluies), c.1881–6, oil on canvas, 180 x 114 cm, National Gallery, London. (Reproduced by courtesy of the Trustees, The National Gallery, London.)

Colour Plate 96.   Georg Friedrich Kersting, Man Reading, 1814, oil on canvas, 47.5 x 37 cm, Oskar Reinhart Collection, Winterthur.

Colour Plate 97.   Rembrandt van Rijn, Lucretia, 1666, oil on canvas, 106 x 92 cm, Minneapolis Institute of Arts, The William Hood Dunwoody Fund.

Colour Plate 98.   Sophonisba Anguissola, Bernardino Campi paints Sophonisba Anguissola, c.1555–60, oil on canvas, (before restoration), 111 x 110 cm, Pinacoteca Nazionale, Siena.

Colour Plate 99. Elisabeth-Louise Vigée-Lebrun, Self-portrait, 1790, oil on canvas, 100 x 81 cm, Galleria degli Uffizi, Florence.

Colour Plate 100. Elisabeth-Louise Vigée-Lebrun, Self-portrait, 1791, oil on canvas, 99 x 81 cm, Ickworth, Suffolk.
(Photograph: The National Trust Photographic Library/Angelo Hornak.)

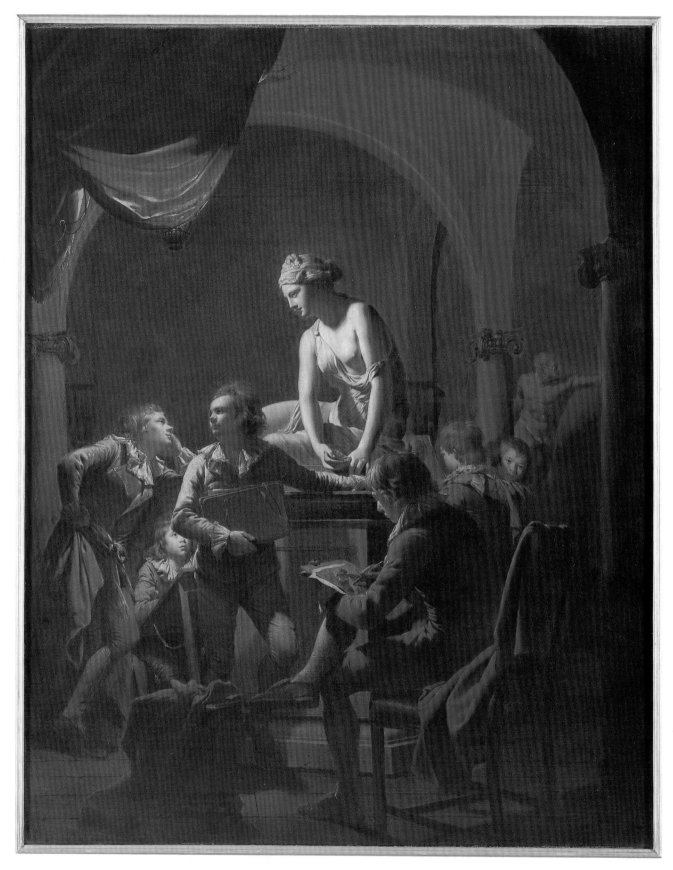

Colour Plate 101. Joseph Wright of Derby, An Academy by Lamplight, c.1768–9, oil on canvas, 127 x 101 cm, Yale Center for British Art, Paul Mellon Collection.

Colour Plate 102. Adélaïde Labille-Guiard, Self-portrait with Two Pupils, 1785, oil on canvas, 210.8 x 151.1 cm.
The Metropolitan Museum of Art, New York. Gift of Julia A. Berwind, 1953 (53.225.5).
(Photograph: © 1980 The Metropolitan Museum of Art.)

Colour Plate 103. Diego Velázquez de Silva, The Kitchen Maid with the Supper at Emmaus, c.1618, oil on canvas, 55 x 118 cm. NGI Cat. No. 4538 (Beit Collection).
(Reproduction courtesy of National Gallery of Ireland.)

Colour Plate 104. Gustave Courbet, After Dinner at Ornans, 1848–49, oil on canvas, 195 x 257 cm. Musée des Beaux-Arts, Lille. (Photograph: Copyright R.M.N. – P. Bernard.)

Colour Plate 105. Pieter de Hooch, Courtyard of a house in Delft, 1658, oil on canvas, 73.5 x 60 cm. National Gallery, London. (Photograph: Copyright Bridgeman Art Library, London.)

Colour Plate 106. Titian, Venus with a Mirror, c.1555, oil on canvas, 124.5 cm x 105.5 cm. Andrew W. Mellon Collection. (Photograph: © 2000 Board of Trustees, National Gallery of Art, Washington.)

Colour Plate 107. Claude Lorraine, Landscape with the Adoration of the Golden Calf, 1660, oil on canvas, 112.8 x 156.6 cm. Manchester City Art Gallery. (Copyright Manchester City Art Galleries.)

Colour Plate 108.   Nicolas Poussin, The Rape of the Sabines, c.1637, 157 x 203 cm. Louvre, Paris. (Photograph: Copyright R.M.N. – P. Bernard.)

Colour Plate 109.   Georges de la Tour, The Penitent Magdalen, 1638–43, oil on canvas, 133.4 x 102.2 cm.
The Metropolitan Museum of Art. Gift of Mr and Mrs Charles Wrightsman, 1978 (1978.517).
(Photograph: © 1997 The Metropolitan Museum of Art.)

Colour Plate 110.   Rembrandt van Rijn, Aristotle with a Bust of Homer, 1653, oil on canvas, 143.5 x 136.5 cm.
The Metropolitan Museum of Art. Purchase, special contributions and funds given or bequeathed by friends of the Museum,
1961 (61.198). (Photograph: © 1993 The Metropolitan Museum of Art.)

Colour Plate 111. Jacob Isaacksz van Ruisdael, Wheatfields, c.1670, oil on canvas, 100 x 130.2 cm. The Metropolitan Museum of Art, bequest of Benjamin Altman, 1913 (14.40.623). (Photograph: ©1994 The Metropolitan Museum of Art.)

Plate 1.   Otto van Veen, The Painter's Family, *1584, oil on canvas, 165 x 250 cm. Musée du Louvre, Paris. (Photograph: © Réunion des Musées Nationaux Documentation Photographique.)*

Plate 2.   Sir William Nicholson, The Hundred Jugs, *1916, oil on canvas, 122 x 152 cm. Walker Art Gallery, Liverpool.*

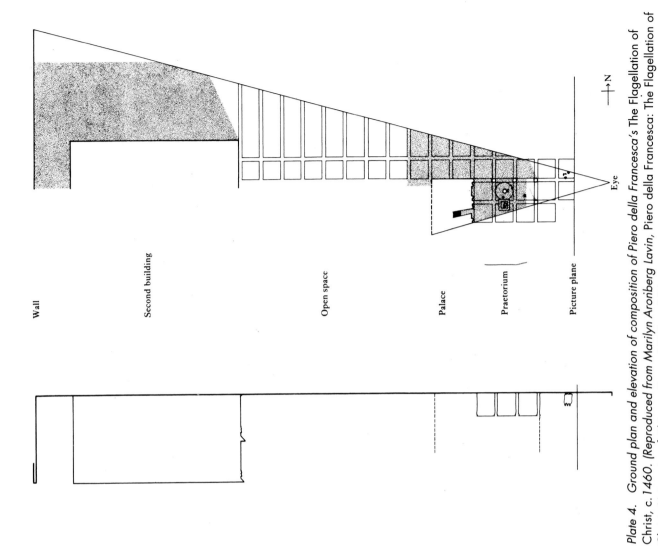

Wall

Second building

Open space

Palace

Praetorium

Picture plane

Eye

→ N

Plate 4.   Ground plan and elevation of composition of Piero della Francesca's The Flagellation of Christ, c.1460. (Reproduced from Marilyn Aronberg Lavin, Piero della Francesca: The Flagellation of Christ, University of Chicago Press, 1972, p.35.)

Plate 3.   Barnett Newman, untitled drawing (also know as The Void), 1946, ink on paper, 45.72 x 60.96 cm. Louisana Museum of Modern Art, Humlebaek, Denmark. (Reproduced by permission of the Barnett Newman Foundation.)

Plate 5. Edgar Degas, Miss La La at the Cirque Fernando, Paris, 1879, oil on canvas, 116.8 x 77.5 cm.
National Gallery, London. (Reproduced by courtesy of the Trustees, The National Gallery, London.)

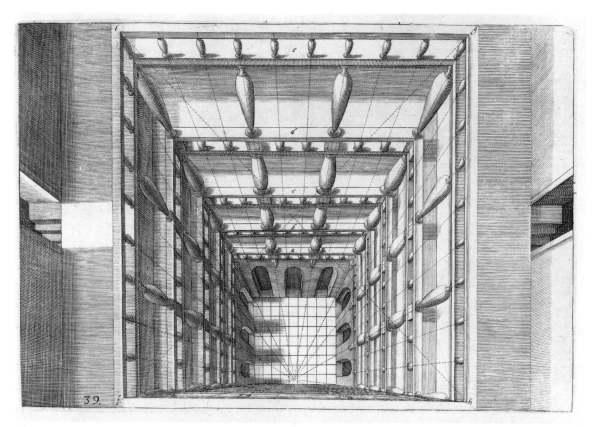

Plate 6. Hans Vredeman de Vries, perspective view, 1604. (Reproduced from J. Vredeman de Vries, Perspective, Leiden, Hondius, 1604–5, pl.39; copyright British Library.)

Plate 7. Walt Disney Studios, background drawing for Clock-Cleaners, 1937. (Reproduced in Christopher Finch, The Art of Walt Disney, New York, Abrams, 1973, p.147; © Disney Enterprises, Inc.)

Plate 8. Daniel Vosmaer, Loggia with a View of Delft, 1663, oil on canvas, 90.5 x 113 cm. Gemeente Musea Delft, Collection Stedelijk Het Prinsenhof, on loan of the Rijksdienst Beeldende Kunst. (Photograph: Tom Haartsen.)

Plate 9.   Rembrandt van Rijn, Portrait of Agatha Bas, 1641, oil on canvas, 104 x 82 cm. Buckingham Palace, London, Royal Collection (1157). (© Her Majesty Queen Elizabeth II.)

Plate 10.   Rembrandt van Rijn, Portrait of Nicolaes van Bambeeck, 1641, oil on canvas, 109 x 83 cm. Royal Museum of Fine Art, Brussels (367). (© ACL; photograph: Musées Royaux des Beaux-Arts de Belgique.)

Plate 11.   Eugene Delacroix, The Return of Christopher Columbus, *1839, oil on canvas, 85.1 x 115.6 cm. Toledo Museum of Art, gift of Thomas A. DeVilbiss (1938.80).*

Plate 12.   John Constable, Wivenhoe Park, Essex, *1816, oil on canvas, 56 x 101 cm. National Gallery of Art, Washington, D.C., Widener Collection. (© 1996 Board of Trustees, The National Gallery of Art, Washington, D.C.)*

Plate 13. Jan Steen, The Life of Man, c. 1665–7, oil on canvas, 68.2 x 82 cm. Mauritshuis, The Hague.

Plate 14. Adriaen van Utrecht, Still Life with White Swan, 1642, oil, 221 x 307 cm. Museo del Prado, Madrid.

Plate 15. Jacques Linard, Still Life with the Five Senses and the Four Elements, 1638, oil, 48 x 60 cm. Musée du Louvre, Paris. (Photograph: © Réunion des Musées Nationaux Documentation Photographique.)

Plate 16.   Albrecht Dürer, Adam and Eve, 1504, engraving, 25 x 18.42 cm. Metropolitan Museum of Art, New York, Fletcher Fund, 1919 (19.73.1).

Plate 17. Sandro Botticelli, The Madonna and Child with Pomegranate, *altarpiece, 1487, tempera on panel, 143.5 cm diameter. Uffizi, Florence. (Photograph: Alinari.)*

Plate 18. Domenico Veneziano, The Annunciation, predella panel, c.1445, tempera on panel, 27 x 54 cm. Fitzwilliam Museum, Cambridge. (Reproduced by permission of the Syndics of The Fitzwilliam Museum, Cambridge.)

Plate 19. Domenico Veneziano, altarpiece with The Virgin and Child with Saints *(St Lucy Altarpiece), central panel, c.1450,
tempera on panel, 209 x 216 cm. Uffizi, Florence. (Photograph: Alinari.)*

Plate 20. Gerard Dou, A Painter in his Studio, c. 1630, oil on panel, 53 x 64.5 cm. Collection Noortman Gallery, Maastricht.

Plate 21. Louise Moillon, The Seller of Fruits and Vegetables, 1630, oil on panel, 120 x 160 cm. Musée du Louvre, Paris. (Photograph: © Lauros–Giraudon.)

Plate 22.   Paul Cézanne, Grounds of the Chateau Noir, 1900–6, oil on canvas, 90.7 x 71.4 cm. National Gallery, London. (Reproduced by courtesy of the Trustees, The National Gallery, London.)

Plate 23. City of Birmingham Symphony Orchestra. (Photograph: Keith Saunders.)

Plate 23 detail (a). French horns. (Photograph: Keith Saunders.)

Plate 23 detail (b). Clarinets and bassoons. (Photograph: Keith Saunders.)

Plate 24. Scene showing the Colosseum. (Reproduced from Goscinny and Uderzo, Obelix and Co., translated by A. Bell and D. Hockridge, Asterix Book 22, Hodder Dargaud, 1976, p.37, by permission of Les Editions Albert René.)

Plate 25. Jean-Léon Gérôme, Pollice Verso, 1872, oil on canvas, 96.5 x 149.2 cm. Phoenix Art Museum, Arizona, purchase.

Plate 26.   C.W. Eckersberg, The Interior of the Colosseum, Rome, *1815, oil on canvas, 34 x 35 cm. Statens Museum for Kunst, Copenhagen (1776).*

Plate 27.   John Singleton Copley, Mr and Mrs Ralph Izard, *1775, oil on canvas, 174.6 x 223.6 cm. Museum of Fine Arts, Boston, Edward Ingersoll Browne Fund. (Courtesy of The Museum of Fine Arts, Boston.)*

Plate 29. Bust of the Emperor Commodus as Hercules, c.192 CE, marble. Capitoline Museum, Rome. (Photograph: Alinari.)

Plate 28. Production of Verdi's Aida in Verona amphitheatre. (Photograph: J. Allan Cash.)

Plate 30.   Maarten van Heemskerck, Self-portrait with the Colosseum, 1553, oil on panel, 42 x 54 cm. Fitzwilliam Museum, Cambridge. (Reproduced by permission of the Syndics of The Fitzwilliam Museum, Cambridge.)

Plate 31.   Gladiator fight, fourth century CE, mosaic, from a villa close to Tuscolo near Rome. Galleria Borghese, Rome. (Photograph: Alinari-Anderson.)

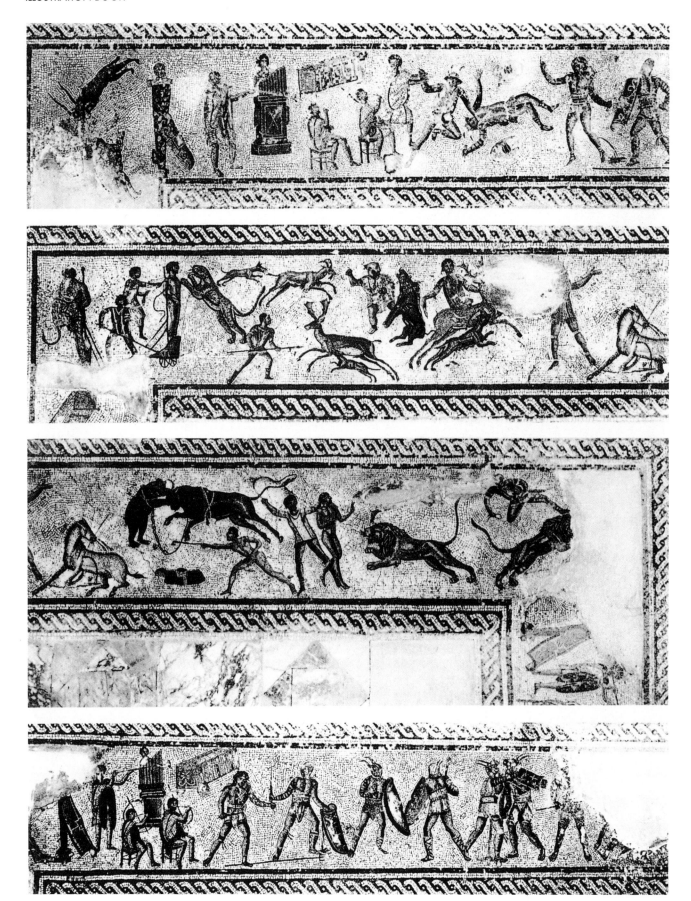

Plate 32. *Gladiators, early third century* CE, *mosaic frieze, room D of villa at Dar Buc Ammera, east of Lepcis Magna, Zliten, Libya. (Photograph: German Archaeological Institute, Rome.)*

Plate 33. Gladiators, third century CE, mosaic, from a site near Madrid. Museo Arqueologico Nacional, Madrid.

Plate 34. Amphitheatre scene, third century CE, mosaic, Sollertiana Domus, El Djem, Tunisia. (Photograph: German Archaeological Institute, Rome.)

Plate 35. Gladiators, third century CE, relief, limestone, from Tomis, Romania.
(Reproduced from J.C. Golvin and C. Landes, Amphithéâtres et gladiateurs, Paris,
Les Presses du CNRS, 1990, p.166; photograph: Robert Landes.)

Plate 36. Graffiti outside House of Trebius Valens, Via Dell' Abbondanza, Pompeii. (Photograph: German
Archaeological Institute, Rome.)

Plate 37. Two female gladiators, early third century CE, inscribed relief, stone, from Halicarnassus. British Museum, London. (Reproduced by permission of the Trustees of The British Museum.)

Plate 38. Ship with crates of wild animals, third century CE, relief, limestone, Villa Medici, Rome. (Photograph: Index/ Fotografia Vasari, Rome.)

Plate 39. Scenes from the arena, early third century CE, floor mosaic, Roman Villa, Nennig, Germany. (Reproduced from Klaus Parlasca, Die Römischen Mosaiken in Deutschland, Berlin, Verlag Walter de Gruyter, 1959.)

Plate 40.   Helmet, first century CE, iron, from Pompeii. Naples Museum.
(Photograph: Index/Luciano Pedicini/Archivio dell' Arte.)

Plate 41.   Parade armour, arm piece and shoulder piece, first century CE, bronze,
from Pompeii. Musée du Louvre, Paris.

(a)

(b)

Plate 42. Colosseum, Rome, corridors and landings: (a) third and fourth storeys, interior view; (b) corridor of second storey. (Photographs: American Academy in Rome Photographs Archive.)

Plate 44. *Renaissance drawings of stuccoes in entrances to Colosseum. (Reproduced from Hermann Egger, Codex Escurialensis, Ein Skizzenbuch aus der Werkstatt Domenico Ghirlandaio, Vienna, Verlag A. Holder, 1906.)*

Plate 43. *Colosseum, Rome, buttress. (Photograph: Colin Cunningham.)*

Plate 45. Colosseum, Rome, points of attachment for sun-shade. (Photograph: Index/Fotografia Vasari, Rome.)

Plate 46. Nineteenth-century photograph of arena. (Photograph: German Archaeological Institute, Rome.)

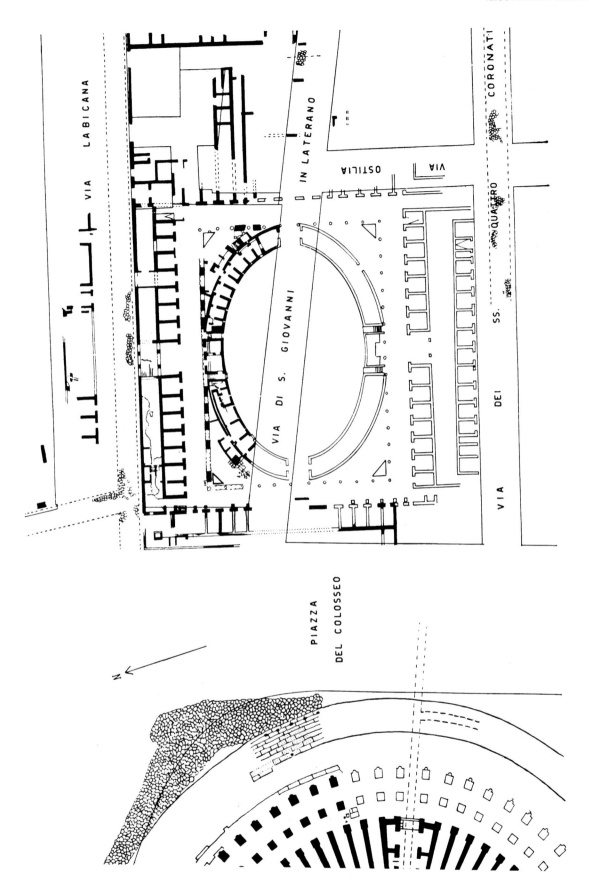

Plate 47. Plan showing the gladiators' training school (Ludus Magnus) in relation to the Colosseum, based on the 1960–1 excavations. (Reproduced from E. Nash, Pictorial Dictionary of Ancient Rome, revised edn, London, Thames & Hudson, 1968, vol.II, p.24, fig.698.)

Plate 48. *Colosseum, Rome, corridor below arena. (Photograph: American Academy in Rome Photographs Archive.)*

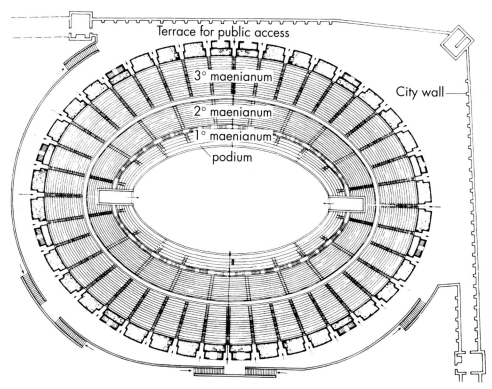

Plate 49. *Amphitheatre, Pompeii, plan, 70–65 BCE. (Reproduced from J.C. Golvin and C. Landes,* Amphithéâtres et gladiateurs, *Paris, Les Presses du CNRS, 1990, p.50.)*

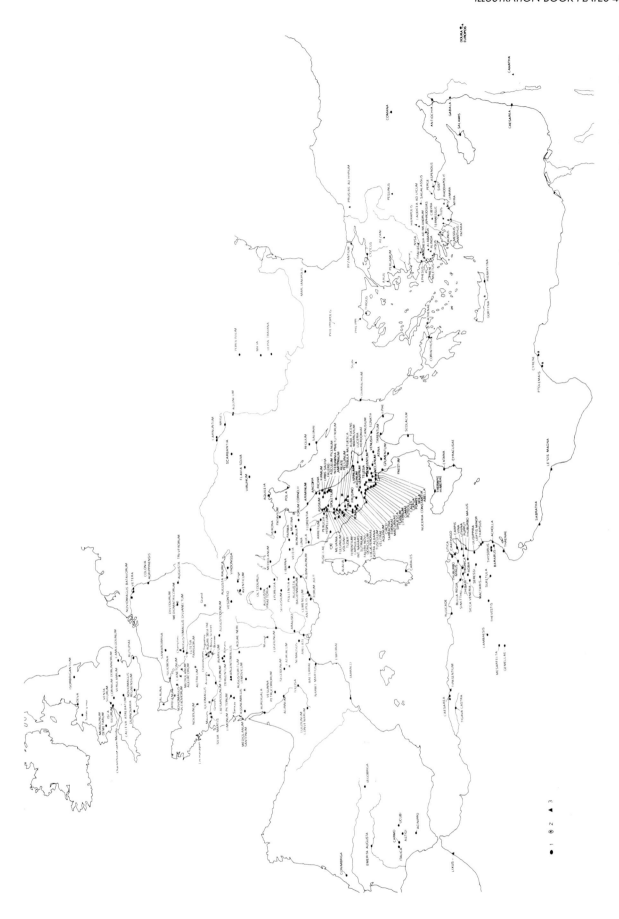

Plate 50. Map showing distribution of amphitheatres throughout Roman world. Key: 1 = amphitheatres (a type found in Roman Gaul); 2 = semi-amphitheatres; 3 = theatre-amphitheatres (usually formed by the adaptation of existing theatre buildings to take gladiatorial games). (Reproduced from J.C. Golvin and C. Landes, Amphithéâtres et gladiateurs, Paris, Les Presses du CNRS, Paris, pp.8–9.)

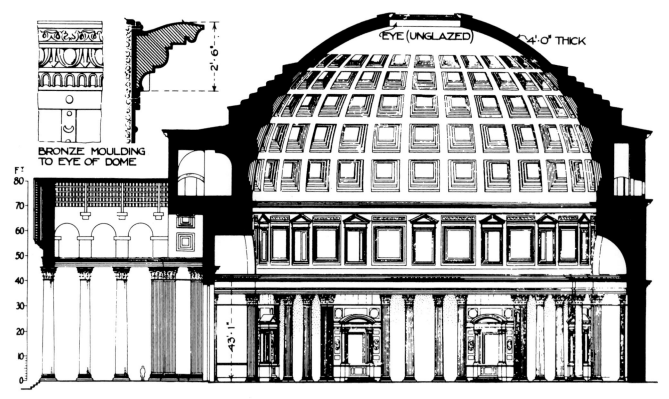

BRONZE MOULDING
TO EYE OF DOME

EYE (UNGLAZED)   4'·0" THICK

Plate 51. Pantheon, Rome, section. (Reproduced from Sir Banister Fletcher's A History of Architecture, © British Architectural Library, The Royal Institute of British Architects.)

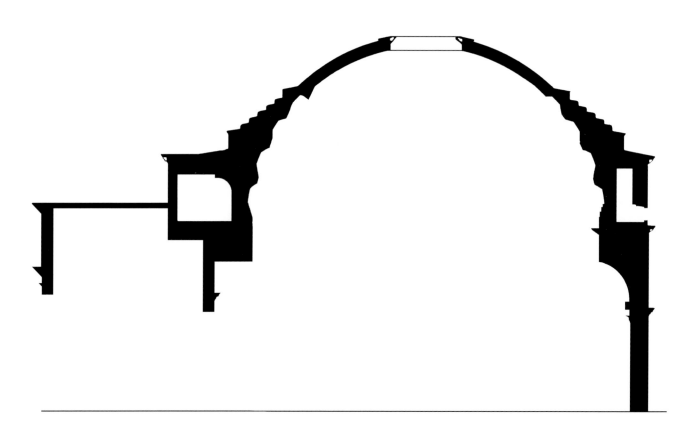

Plate 52. Pantheon, Rome, section. (Adapted from Sir Banister Fletcher's A History of Architecture, © British Architectural Library, The Royal Institute of British Architects.)

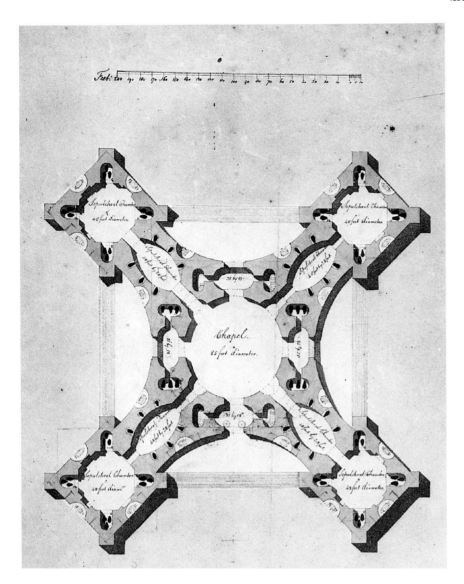

Plate 53.   Sir John Soane, plan of a mausoleum, c.1780. Sir John Soane's Museum, London (45/1/16). (Reproduced by courtesy of the Trustees of Sir John Soane's Museum.)

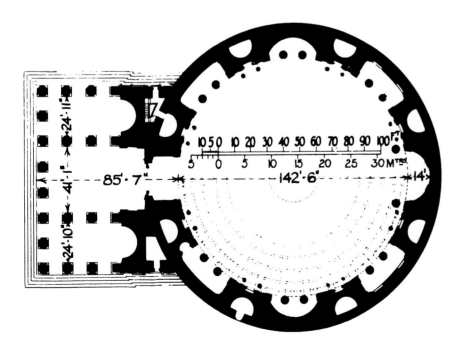

Plate 54.   Pantheon, Rome, plan. (Reproduced from Sir Banister Fletcher's A History of Architecture, © British Architectural Library, The Royal Institute of British Architects.)

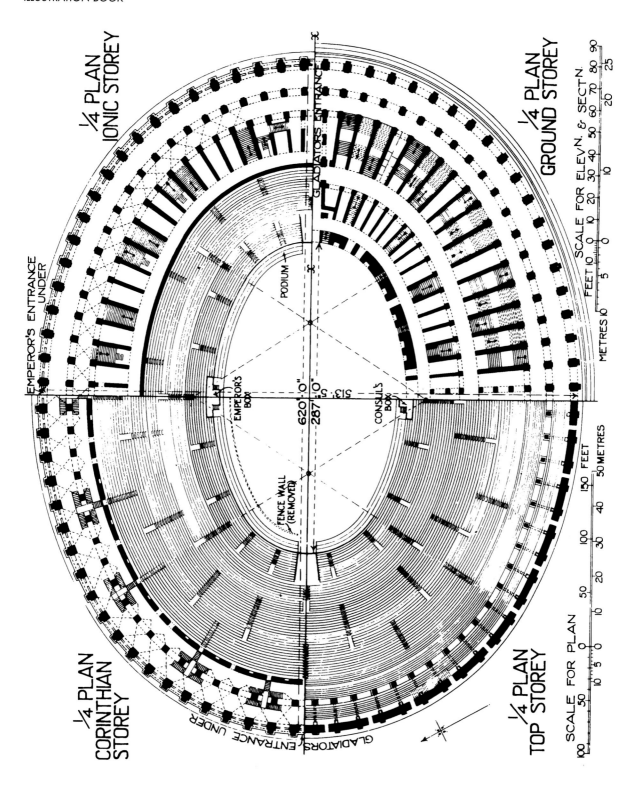

Plate 55. Colosseum, Rome, plan. (Reproduced from Sir Banister Fletcher's A History of Architecture, © British Architectural Library, The Royal Institute of British Architects.)

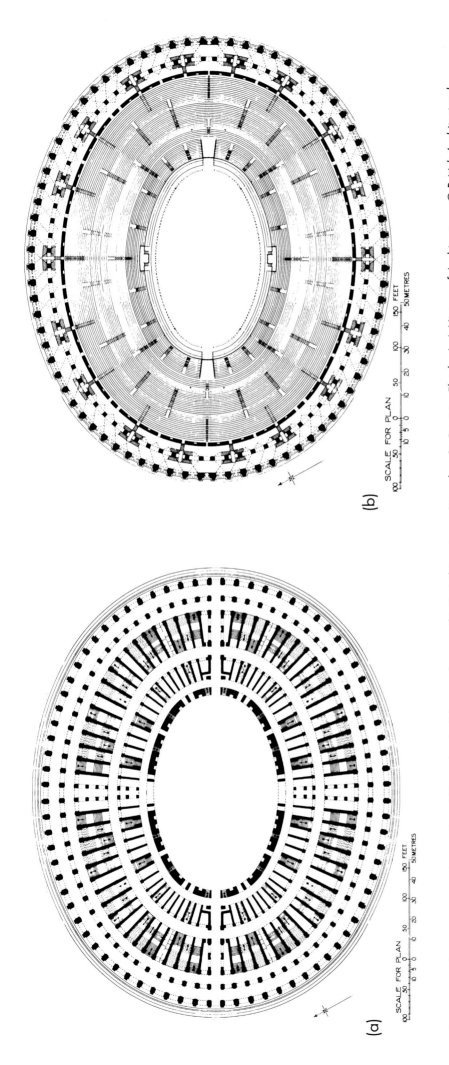

(b)

SCALE FOR PLAN

(a)

SCALE FOR PLAN

Plate 56. Colosseum, Rome, plans at four different levels: (a) ground storey; (b) Corinthian storey. (Based on Sir Banister Fletcher's A History of Architecture, © British Architectural Library, The Royal Institute of British Architects.) [cont. overleaf]

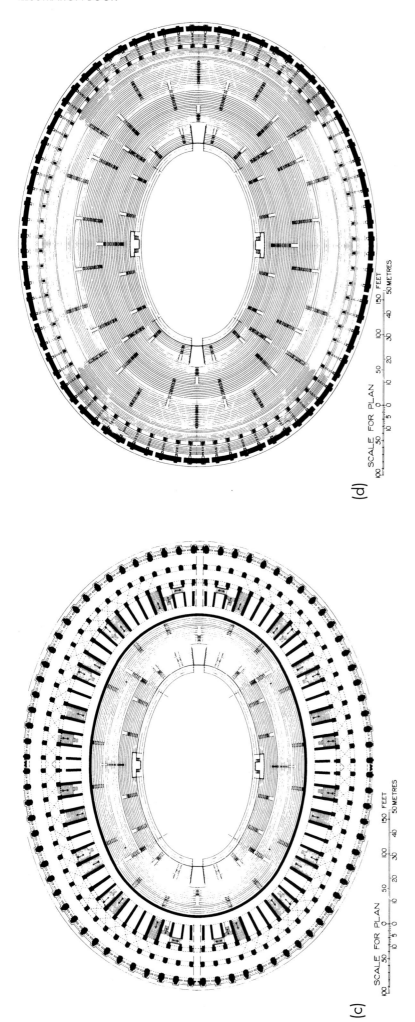

SCALE FOR PLAN

(d)

SCALE FOR PLAN

(c)

Plate 56 (cont.). Colosseum, Rome, plans at four different levels: (c) Ionic storey; (d) top storey. (Based on Sir Banister Fletcher's A History of Architecture, © British Architectural Library, The Royal Institute of British Architects.)

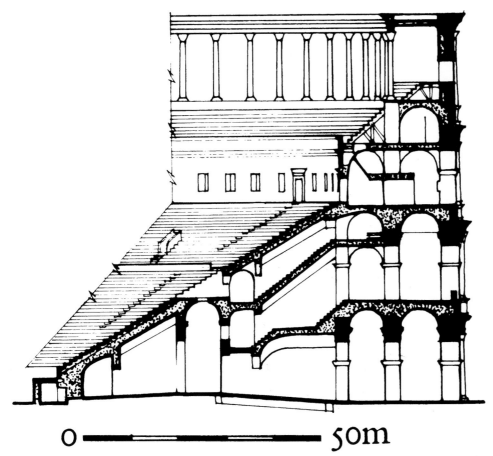

Plate 57. Colosseum, Rome, section. (Reproduced from J.B. Ward-Perkins, Roman Imperial Architecture, London, Penguin, 1981; © Penguin Books.)

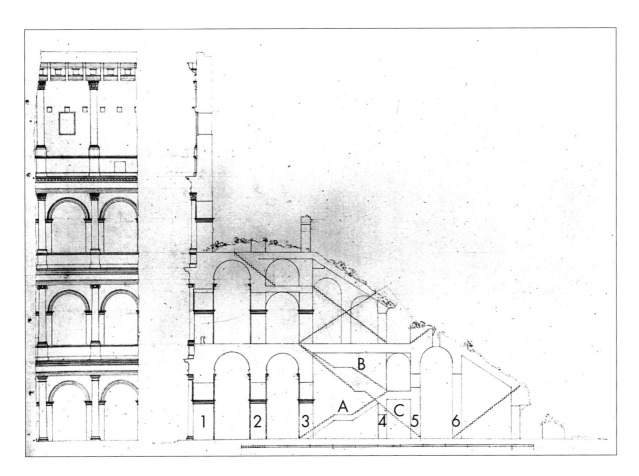

Plate 58. Sir John Soane, Colosseum, Rome, diagrammatic section and part elevation, 1778–80. Sir John Soane's Museum, London (20/5/7). (Reproduced by courtesy of the Trustees of Sir John Soane's Museum.)

Plate 59. Colosseum, Rome. (Photograph: Alinari-Brogi.)

Plate 60.   Bramante, Tempietto San Pietro in Montorio, Rome, 1502. (Photograph: Alinari-Anderson.)

Plate 61. President Nicolae Ceausescu's Palace, Bucharest, 1970s and 1980s. (Photograph: Greg Evans International/Monica Evans.)

Plate 62. Mies van der Rohe and Philip Johnson, Seagram Building, New York, 1958. (Photograph: Ezra Stoller C.ESTO).

Plate 63.   Half-timbered farmhouse, Grange Farm, Abbey Dore, Herefordshire, fourteenth century and later.
(© Crown copyright; photograph: National Monuments Record, RCHME.)

Plate 64.   Piers Gough of CZWG, Bryanston School, CDT building, 1987–8 (Photograph: Colin Cunningham.)

Plate 65. Arch of Titus, Rome, c.81 CE. (Photograph: Alinari-Anderson.)

Plate 66. *Canterbury Cathedral, predominantly 1175–84, rebuilt 1391–1468 with central tower 1494–1503 and later additions, from the south-west. (Photograph: A.F. Kersting.)*

Plate 67. *Ictinus and Kallikrates, Parthenon, Athens, 447–36 BCE. (Photograph: Hirmer Verlag, Munich.)*

Plate 68. C.R. Cockerell, Ashmolean Museum, Oxford, 1841–5. (Photograph: A.F. Kersting.)

Plate 69. Giulio Romano, Palazzo del Te, Mantua, 1525 onwards. (Photograph: Logos di Guariento e Selin, Mantua.)

Plate 70.   Louis le Vau and Claude Perrault, Louvre, Paris, east façade, 1667. (Photograph: A.F. Kersting.)

Plate 71.   George Steuart, Attingham Park, Shropshire, 1782. (Photograph: A.F. Kersting.)

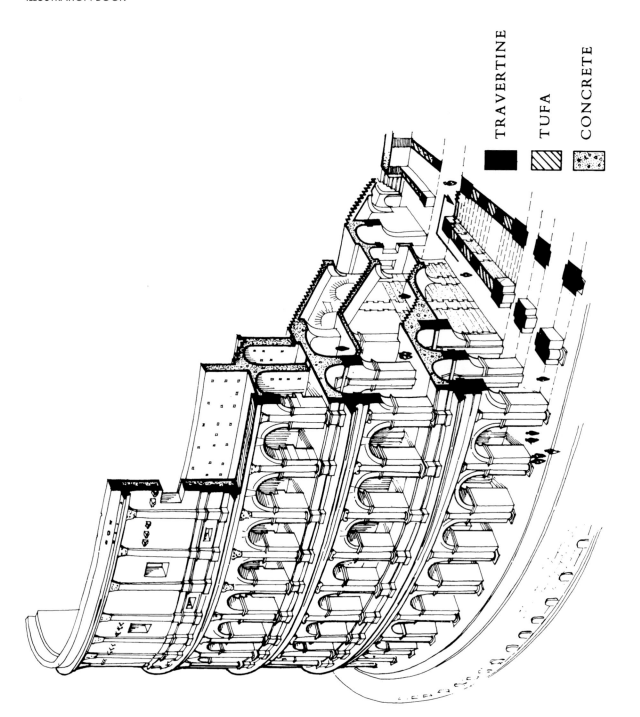

TRAVERTINE

TUFA

CONCRETE

Plate 72.   Colosseum, Rome, section, showing stairs and arcades.   (Reproduced from J.B. Ward-Perkins, Roman Imperial Architecture, London, Penguin, 1981; © Penguin Books.)

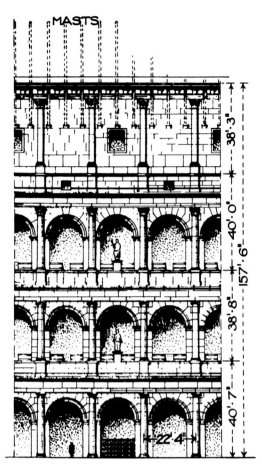

Plate 73. Colosseum, Rome, elevation. (Reproduced from Sir Banister Fletcher's A History of Architecture, © British Architectural Library, The Royal Institute of British Architects.)

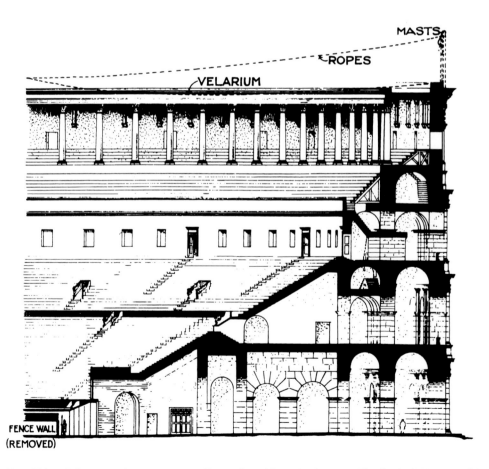

Plate 74. Colosseum, Rome, section. (Reproduced from Sir Banister Fletcher's A History of Architecture, © British Architectural Library, The Royal Institute of British Architects.)

Plate 75. Colosseum, Rome, exterior, showing the three orders. (Photograph: Colin Cunningham.)

Plate 76. Colosseum, Rome, exterior, Corinthian arcade. (Photograph: Colin Cunningham.)

Plate 77.   Colosseum, Rome, view of interior arcade looking along ambulatory. (Photograph: Alinari-Anderson.)

Plate 78. Sir John Soane, Colosseum, Rome, elevation of section, 1778–80. Sir John Soane's Museum, London (45/3/50). (Reproduced by courtesy of the Trustees of Sir John Soane's Museum.)

Plate 79. Colosseum, Rome, with articulation removed from right-hand portion. (Based on data of Plate 59.)

Plate 80.   Museum of Roman Civilization (Museo della Civiltà Romana), Rome, 1939–40, designed for Mussolini's abortive International Exhibition E'42, by the architects F. Guerri, E. Lapadula and G. Romano. (Photograph: Alinari.)

Plate 81.   Sultan Han, near Kayseri, Turkey, thirteenth century, main façade. (Photograph: Sonia Halliday.)

Plate 82.   Great Mosque at Samarra, Iraq, 848 onwards. (Photograph: British Architectural Library Photographic Collection, RIBA, London.)

Plate 83. Juan Bautista de Toledo, El Escorial, Madrid, 1562–82, exterior west façade. (Photograph: A.F. Kersting.)

Plate 84. Sir Robert Smirke, British Museum, London, 1823–46. (Photograph: A.F. Kersting.)

Plate 85. John Nash, Cumberland Terrace, London, 1812–13. (Photograph: A.F. Kersting.)

Plate 87. Philip Hardwick, Euston Arch, London, 1835–7. (Photograph: A.F. Kersting.)

Plate 86. Cuthbert Brodrick, Leeds Town Hall, 1853–9. (Photograph: A.F. Kersting.)

Plate 88.   Porta Nigra, Trier, Germany, early fourth century CE. (Photograph: A.F. Kersting.)

Plate 89.   Amphitheatre, Arles, late first century CE. (Photograph: Giraudon.)

Plate 91. Giovanni Lorenzo Bernini, St Peter's Square, Rome, 1656 onwards, part of colonnade. (Photograph: A.F. Kersting.)

Plate 90. Church of the Intercession on the Nerl, Bogolyubovo, 1165. (Photograph: Klaus G. Beyer, Weimar.)

Plate 92.   Leon Battista Alberti, Palazzo Rucellai, Florence, 1453 onwards. (Photograph: A.F. Kersting.)

Plate 93. Andrea Palladio, Basilica, Vicenza, 1459 onwards. (Photograph: British Architectural Library Photographs Collection, RIBA, London.)

Plate 94. Cabildo, New Orleans, 1795 onwards. (Photograph: © Wayne Andrews/Esto. All rights reserved.)

Plate 95. James Hoban, The White House, Washington, D.C., 1792–1829 (Photograph: J. Allan Cash.)

Plate 96. Chevron Barracks, Colombo, Sri Lanka, late nineteenth century. (Photograph: British Architectural Library Photographs Collection, RIBA, London.)

Plate 97. John Nash, Park Crescent, London, 1812 onwards. (Photograph: A.F. Kersting.)

Plate 98.   Bull ring, Plaza de Toros Ronda, Malaga, Spain, 1784. (Photograph: J. Allan Cash.)

Plate 99. Newcastle United Football Ground, St James's Park, 1906, west stand, exterior. (Photograph: City Library, Newcastle-upon-Tyne, Local Studies; photograph dated 1975.)

Plate 100. Newcastle United Football Ground, St James's Park, interior, west stand on left. (Photograph: City Library, Newcastle-upon-Tyne, Local Studies; photograph dated 1975.)

Plate 101. Taylor, Tulip & Hunter, Newcastle United Football Ground, St James's Park, new north stand, 1992. (Reproduced by courtesy of Taylor, Tulip, Hunter Associates.)

Plate 102.   Robin Lobb & Partners, Alfred MacAlpine Stadium, Huddersfield, 1994. (Reproduced by courtesy of Kirklees Stadium Development Ltd.)

Plate 103.   Werner March, Olympiastadion, Berlin, 1934–6. (Photograph: Bildarchiv Foto Marburg.)

Plate 104.   Heysel Stadium, Brussels, 1930, main entrance. (Photograph: Archives de la Ville de Bruxelles (11611).)

Plate 105. *Albert Speer, Floodlights at Olympic Games, Olympiastadion, Berlin, 16 August 1936, drawing by H. Liska.* (Photograph: Bildarchiv Preussischer Kulturbesitz Berlin.)

Plate 106. Hampden Park, Glasgow, 1930s, terraces. (Photograph: Sporting Pictures (UK).)

Plate 107. Portsmouth Football Ground, Fratton Park, 1905, entrance. (Reproduced by courtesy of Portsmouth Football Club.)

Plate 108.   Valley Parade Ground, Bradford, 1908, main stand. (Photograph: John Dewhirst.)

Plate 109.   Maxwell Ayrton, Derby City Football Ground, design for a new stadium incorporating a health centre, 1945.
(Reproduced by courtesy of The British Architectural Library, RIBA, London.)

Plate 110. Blackpool, stand with timber frame and steel supports for roof, c.1917. (Reproduced by courtesy of Blackpool Football Club.)

Plate 111. Roger Taillebert, Parc des Princes, Paris, 1967–70. (Photograph: SIPFA/Rex Features.)

Plate 112.   Pier Luigi Nervi, Stadio Communale, Florence, 1930–2. (Photograph: Alinari.)

Plate 113. Wembley Stadium, showing supports for roof, Arsenal v. Manchester United, FA Charity Shield, 7 August 1993. (Photograph: Colorsport.)

Plate 114. Wembley Stadium, 1924 and later, view of twin towers and main entrance. (Photograph: Wembley Stadium Ltd.)

Plate 115.   Ferrucio Calzolari and Armando Ronca, San Siro III, Milan, 1989. (Photograph: Index/Olympia Fotocronache.)

Plate 116.   Wembley, British Empire Exhibition, Australian Pavilion and Stadium. (Reproduced from D.R. Knight, The Lion Roars at Wembley, 1984, by permission of the author.)

Plate 117. Wembley, British Empire Exhibition, view of the Palace of Industries and Stadium. (Reproduced from D.R. Knight, The Lion Roars at Wembley, 1984, by permission of the author.)

Plate 118. Wembley, British Empire Exhibition, view of the Government Pavilion. (Reproduced from D.R. Knight, The Lion Roars at Wembley, 1984, by permission of the author.)

Plate 119. Wembley Stadium, view of interior. (Photograph: Wembley Stadium Ltd.)

Plate 120. Wembley Stadium, detail of tower.
(Photograph: Wembley Stadium Ltd.)

Plate 122.   Wembley Stadium, new players' tunnel, 1948 and later additions. (Photograph: Colin Cunningham.)

Plate 121.   Wembley Stadium, view of side arch and access stairs. (Photograph: Colin Cunningham.)

Plate 123.   Wembley Stadium, crowded terraces and royal box, FA Cup Final 1953. (Photograph: Colorsport.)

Plate 124. Sir Owen Williams, Wembley Stadium, 1922–3, view from west. (Photograph: © National Monuments Record, RCHME.)

Plate 125. Milan Arena, 1807. (Photograph: Alinari.)

Plate 126. Jacques-Louis David, The Oath in the Tennis Court, 1790–91, drawing, mixed techniques (ink, wash, chalk over pencil), 66 x 101.2 cm. Musée du Louvre, Paris. (Photograph: © Réunion des Musées Nationaux.)

Plate 127. Jacques-Louis David, The Oath in the Tennis Court, 1790–91, drawing and oil on canvas, mixed techniques, fragment, 358 x 648 cm. Musée National du Chateau, Versailles. (Photograph: © Réunion des Musées Nationaux.)

Plate 128.   Charles-Nicolas Cochin, Academy Figure, *1763, engraving. (Reproduced from Diderot and D'Alembert,* Encyclopédie … recueil des planches II, *Paris, Bibliothèque Nationale de France, 1763.)*

Plate 129. Charles de Wailly, The Salon of 1789 at the Louvre, *1789, detail, drawing, mixed techniques (pierre noire et sanguine), 33.2 x 37.4 cm. Musée Carnavalet, Paris. (Photograph: Bulloz.)*

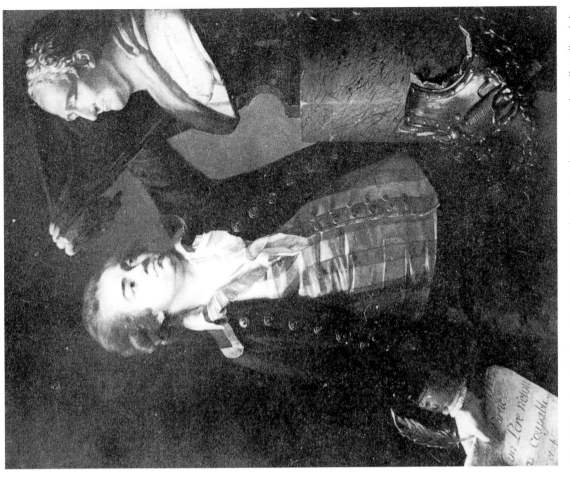

Plate 131. Jean Baptiste Claude Robin, Trophime Girard, Marquis de Lally-Tollendal Unveiling the Bust of his Father, 1787, oil on canvas, 145.5 x 113.5 cm. Private collection.

Plate 130. Jacques-Louis David, Lavoisier and his Wife, 1788, oil on canvas, 259.7 x 194.6 cm. Metropolitan Museum of Art, purchase, Mr and Mrs Charles Wrightsman, gift in honour of Everett Fahy, 1977 (1977.10).

Plate 132. Jacques-Louis David, The Triumph of the French People, 1793–4, pen and Chinese ink wash on paper, 32 × 70 cm. Musée Carnavalet, Paris. (Photograph: Bulloz.)

Plate 133. Pierre-Alexandre Tardieu, engraving after David's Lepelletier de St.-Fargeau, 1793, engraving, 32 x 70 cm. Bibliothèque Nationale de France, Paris, Cabinet des Estampes.

Plate 134. Jacques-Louis David, sketch of Marie Antoinette on her way to execution, 16 October 1793, pen and ink drawing, 15 x 10 cm. Musée du Louvre, Paris (3599). (Photograph: Mansell Collection.)

Plate 135. J. Minot, Playing Cards of the Revolution, *detail of* Brutus, *1794, woodcuts. Musée Carnavalet, Paris. (Photograph: Bulloz.)*

Plate 136. Gavin Hamilton, Oath of Brutus, 1763–4, oil on canvas, 213.3 x 264 cm. Drury Lane Theatre, London. (Photograph: Mike Levers/The Open University.)

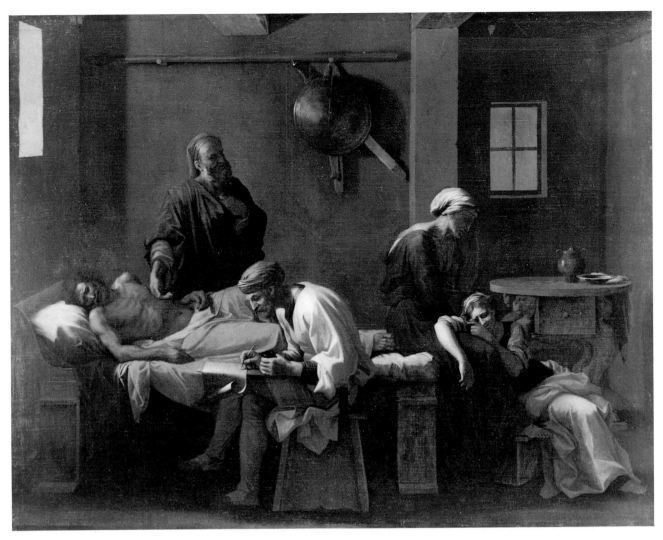

Plate 137. Nicolas Poussin, Testament of Eudamidas, c.1650, oil on canvas, 110.5 x 138.5 cm. Statens Museum for Kunst, Copenhagen.

Plate 139. Jacques-Louis David, tracing after Capitoline Brutus, c. 1784 (?), ink, 22 x 16 cm. Private collection. (Photograph: Yale University Library.)

Plate 138. Capitoline Brutus, late fourth century BC, bronze, Vatican, Rome. (Photograph: Alinari-Anderson.)

Plate 141. Jacques-Louis David, Jupiter, c. 1784 (?), detail, tracing, ink, 14 x 26 cm. Private collection. (Photograph: Yale University Library.)

Plate 140. Seated Philosopher, first century CE, marble, Palazzo Spada, Rome. (Photograph: Alinari.)

Plate 142. Michelangelo, Isaiah, 1508–12, ceiling fresco, Sistine Chapel, Vatican, Rome. (Photograph: Alinari-Anderson.)

Plate 143.   Giotto di Bondone, The Vision of Joachim, 1304–13, fresco, Arena Chapel, Padua. (Photograph: Alinari-Anderson.)

Plate 144. *Niobid Sarcophagus, first century* CE, *detail, marble, Vatican, Rome.* (*Photograph: Alinari-Anderson.*)

Plate 145.   Jacques-Louis David, The Fainting Daughter, 1789, ink drawing, 11 x 12 cm.
Foundation Custodia, Paris.

Plate 146.   Joseph-Marie Vien, La Marchande d'Amours, 1763, oil on canvas, 95 x 118 cm. Palais de
Fontainebleau. (Photograph: Lauros–Giraudon.)

Plate 147. Jacques-Louis David, Brutus and Members of his Household, c.1788, black chalk,
14 x 19 cm. Musée Bonnat, Bayonne. (Photograph: © Réunion des Musées Nationaux – R.G. Ojeda.)

Plate 148. Jacques-Louis David, compositional study for Brutus, c.1788, black and brown chalk on paper,
23.9 x 30.8 cm. Metropolitan Museum of Art, New York, Robert Lehmann Collection, 1978 (1975.1.607).

Plate 149. Jacques-Louis David, compositional study for Brutus, c.1788, black chalk, 21 x 33 cm. Musée Bonnat, Bayonne. (Photograph: © Réunion des Musées Nationaux – R.G. Ojeda.)

Plate 150. Jacques-Louis David, oil study for Brutus, c.1788, oil on canvas, 28 x 36 cm. National Museum, Stockholm. (Photograph: Staten Konstmuseer.)

Plate 152. Jacques-Louis David, Brutus Seated, Head Erect, c.1788, black chalk, 14.3 x 11.1 cm. Musée Bonnat, Bayonne. (Photograph: © Réunion des Musées Nationaux – R.G. Ojeda.)

Plate 151. Jacques-Louis David, The Dejected Brutus, c. 1788, black chalk, 14.3 x 10.5 cm. Musée Bonnat, Bayonne. (Photograph: © Réunion des Musées Nationaux – R.G. Ojeda.)

Plate 154. Caspar David Friedrich, Plant Study for Sketchbook of 1799, pen, 24 x 19 cm. Staatliche Museen, Kupferstichkabinett und Sammlung der Zeichnungen, Berlin. (Photograph: Bildarchiv Berlin Preussischer Kulturbesitz/Jörg P. Anders.)

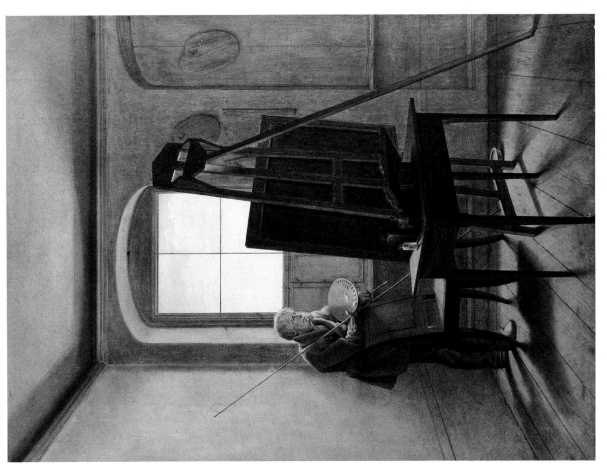

Plate 153. Georg Friedrich Kersting, Caspar David Friedrich in his Studio, c. 1812, oil on canvas, 54 x 42 cm. Staatliche Museen zu Berlin Preussischer Kulturbesitz Alte Nationalgalerie. (Photograph: Jorg P. Anders.)

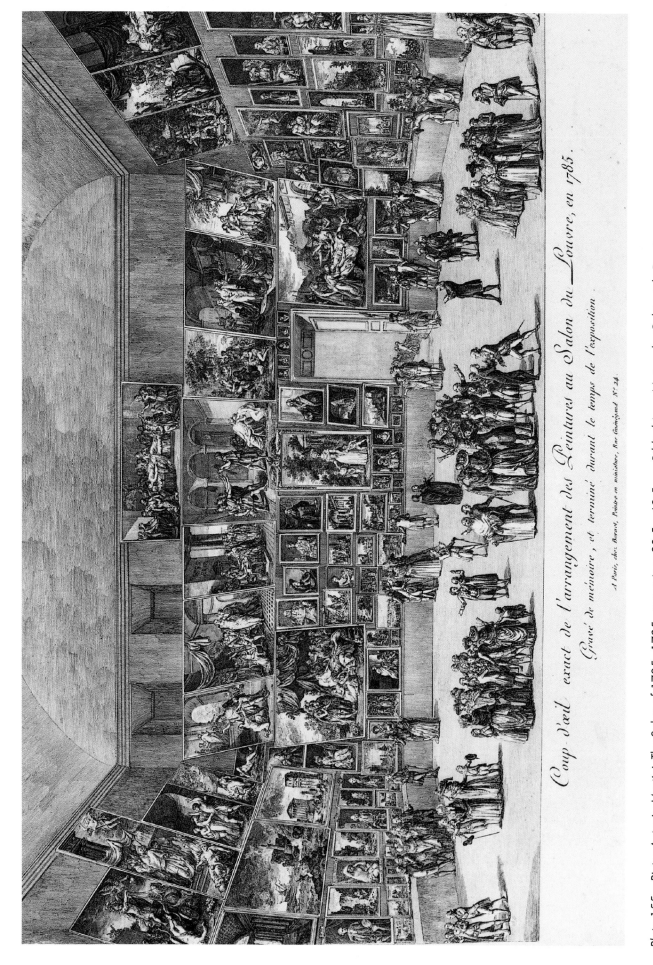

Plate 155.   Pietro Antonio Martini, The Salon of 1785, 1785, engraving, 38.5 x 62.5 cm. Bibliothèque Nationale, Cabinet de Dessins.

Plate 156.   Jean-Baptiste Deshays, The Martyrdom of St Andrew, *centre panel for main altarpiece of church of Saint André-de-la-Porte-aux-Fèvres de Rouen, seized during Revolution, 1759, oil on canvas, 445 x 214 cm. Musée des Beaux-Arts, Rouen.*

Plate 157. J.-B. Suvée, Cornelia, Mother of the Gracchi, 1795, oil on canvas, 320 x 414 cm. Musée du Louvre, Paris. (Photograph: © Réunion des Musées Nationaux.)

Plate 158. Caspar David Friedrich, Procession at Dawn, 1805, pen and sepia, 40 x 62 cm. Staatliche Kunstammlungen, Graphische Sammlung, Weimar.

Plate 159. Nicolas Poussin, Landscape with a Man Killed by a Snake, 1648, oil on canvas, 119.4 x 198.8 cm. National Gallery, London. (Reproduced by courtesy of the Trustees, The National Gallery, London.)

Plate 160 (a). Tithe map of the hamlet of Lantwit Lower in the Parish of Lantwit-juxta-Neath, prepared by Alfred Russel Wallace, 1846. The map is reproduced at 22 per cent of its original size, c. 112 x 78 cm. (Reproduced by permission of Llyfrgell Genedlaethol Cymru/National Library of Wales, Aberystwyth, Department of Maps, C2.)

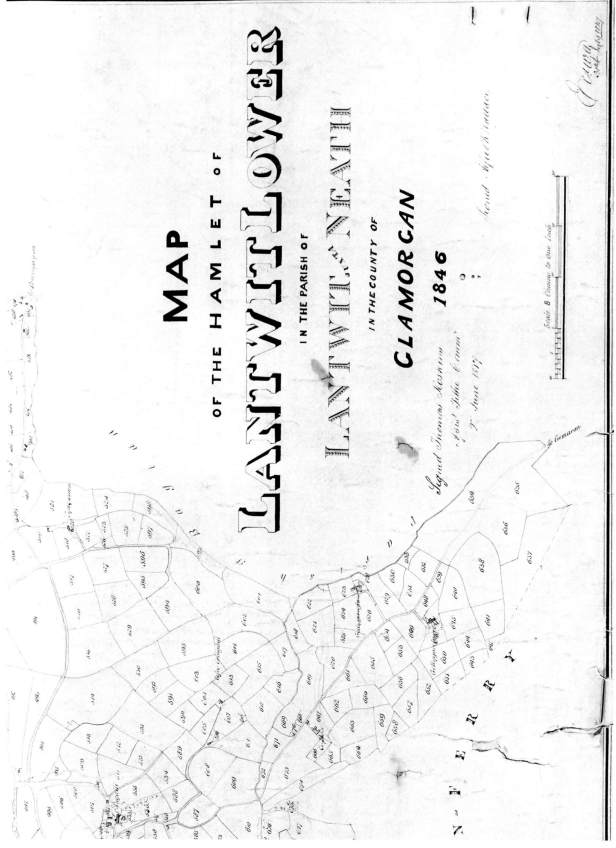

Plate 160 (b).
Detail from Plate 160 (a)
with Wallace's signature.
(Reproduced by permission
of Llyfrgell Genedlaethol
Cymru/National Library
of Wales, Aberystwyth,
Department of Maps, C2.)

LONDON: Printed by John Williams & Co., 29, Bucklersbury.

LANDOWNERS.	OCCUPIERS.	Numbers referring to the Plan.	NAME AND DESCRIPTION or LANDS AND PREMISES.	STATE or CULTIVATION.	QUANTITIES IN STATUTE MEASURE.			Amount of Rent Charge apportioned upon the several Lands, and Payable to the Rector of LLANTWIT JUXTA NEATH.			REMARKS.
					A.	R.	P.	£.	s.	d.	

Plate 160 (c).
A page from Wallace's schedule of fields, some shown in Plate 160 (b).
Reproduced by permission of Llyfrgell Genedlaethol Cymru/National Library of Wales, Aberystwyth, Department of Maps, C2.)

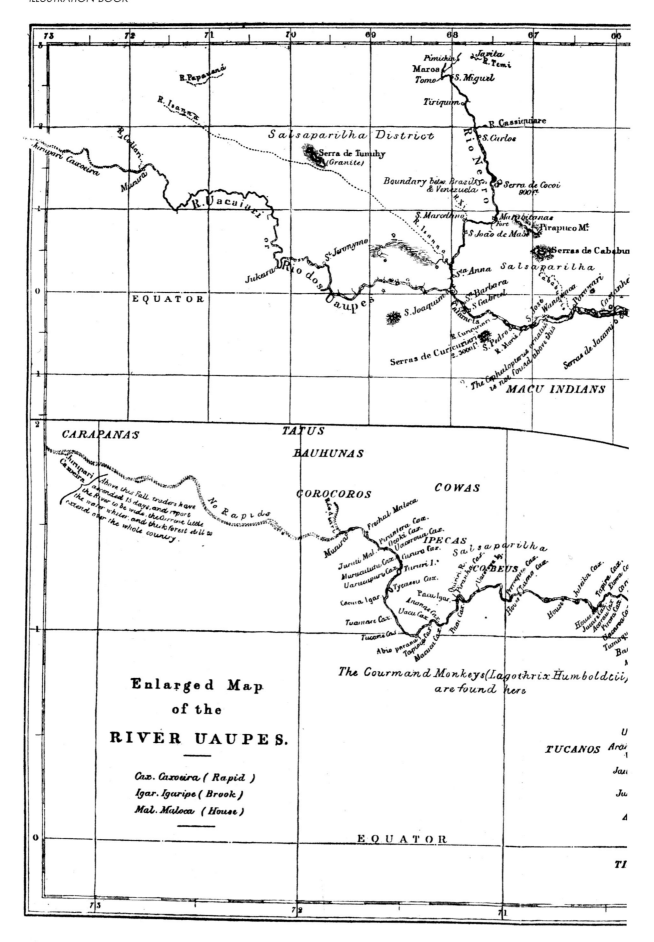

Plate 161.   Map of habitats along the rivers Negro and Uaupés in western Brazil, prepared by Alfred Russel Wallace from observations made in 1851–2. (From Wallace, My Life, 1905, London, Chapman and Hall, vol.1, facing p.320; first published in Journal of the Royal Geographical Society, 1853, vol.23; original manuscript in Royal Geographical Society, London.)

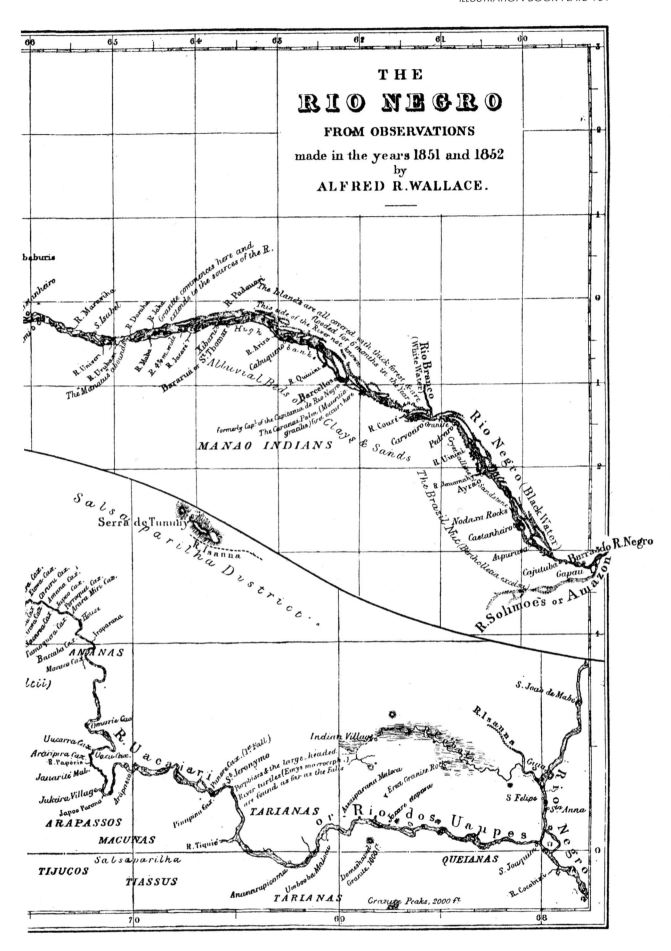

THE
RIO NEGRO
FROM OBSERVATIONS
made in the years 1851 and 1852
by
ALFRED R. WALLACE.

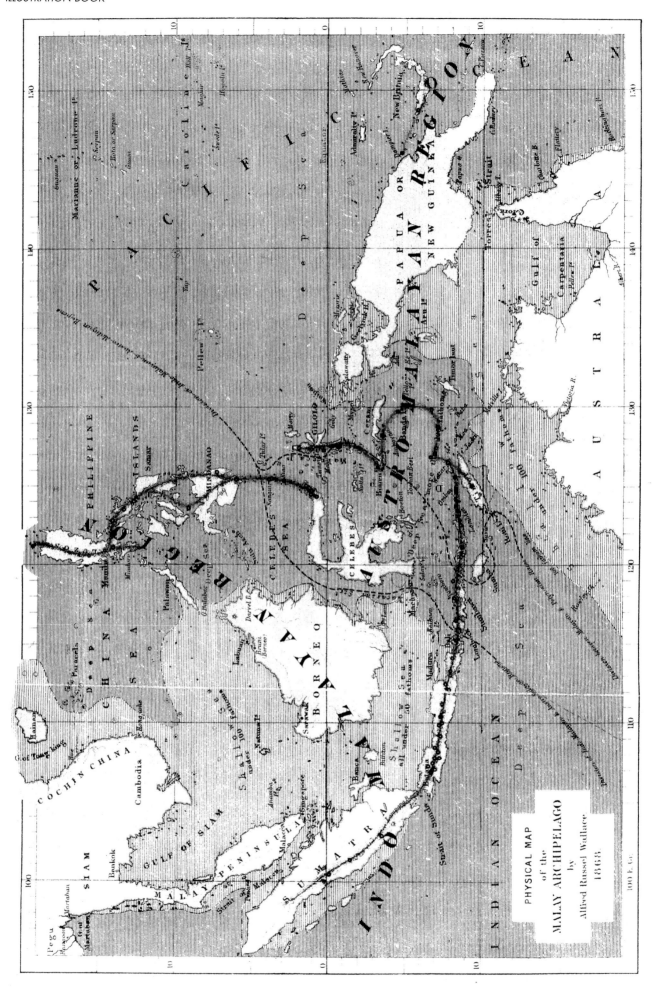

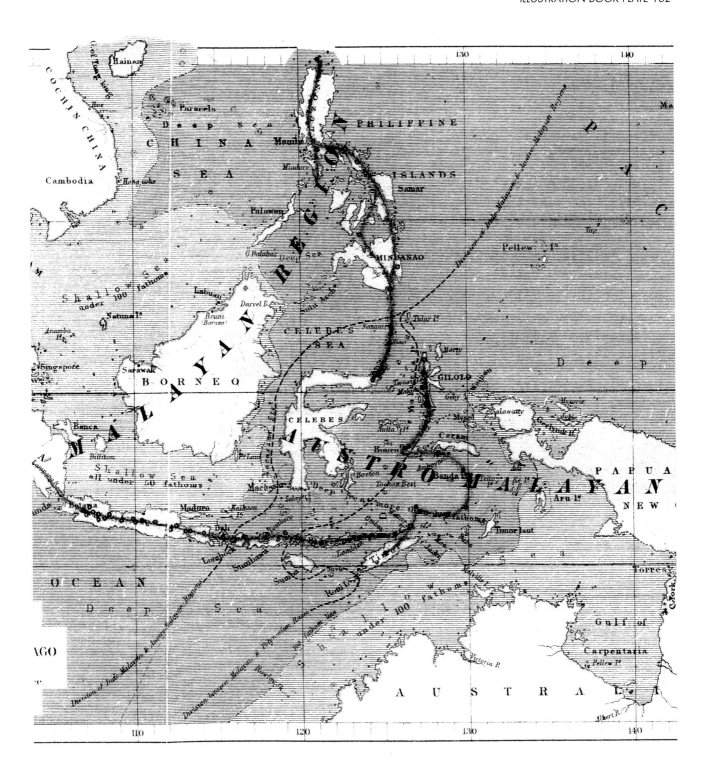

Plate 162 (left) and enlarged detail (above). Map showing faunal and racial boundaries (alongside dark volcanic belts) in the Malay Archipelago, prepared by Alfred Russel Wallace, 1868. (From Wallace, The Malay Archipelago, 6th edn, 1877, London, Macmillan, facing p.9.) He first showed the faunal boundary – 'Wallace's Line' – on a map published in 1863 and he described the racial boundary a year later: 'If we draw a line, commencing on the eastern side of the Philippine Islands, thence along the western of Gilolo, through the island of Bouru, and curving round coast the west end of Flores, then bending back round Sandalwood Island to take in Rotti, we shall divide the archipelago into two portions, the races of which have strongly marked distinctive peculiarities. This line will separate the Malayan and Asiatic from the Papuan and Pacific races, and though along the line of junction intermigration and commixture have taken place, yet the division is on the whole almost as well defined and strongly contrasted as are the corresponding zoological divisions of the archipelago into an Indo-Malayan and Austro-Malayan region' (Wallace, 'On the Varieties of Man in the Malay Archipelago', Transactions of the Ethnological Society of London, new series, 1865, vol.3, p.211).

Boat-building
weapons – starting fires
& competition with other savages.

(tie knots) opening fruit

---

392   Sir Charles Lyell on

tralians or the Andaman islanders, are very little above those of many animals. The higher moral faculties and those of pure intellect and refined emotion are useless to them, are rarely if ever manifested, and have no relation to their wants, desires, or well-being. How, then, was an organ developed so far beyond the needs of its possessor? Natural selection could only have endowed the savage with a brain a little superior to that of an ape, whereas he actually possesses one but very little inferior to that of the average members of our learned societies.

Again, what a wonderful organ is the hand of man;* of what marvels of delicacy is it capable, and how greatly it assists in his education and mental development! The whole circle of the arts and sciences are ultimately dependent on our possession of this organ, without which we could hardly have become truly human. This hand is equally perfect in the lowest savage, but he has no need for so fine an instrument, and can no more fully utilise it than he could use without instruction a complete set of joiner's tools. But, stranger still, this marvellous instrument was foreshadowed and prepared in the Quadrumana; and any person, who will watch how one of these animals uses its hands, will at once perceive that it possesses an organ far beyond its needs. The separate fingers and the thumb are never fully utilised, and objects are grasped so clumsily, as to show that a much less specialised organ of prehension would have served its purpose quite as well; and if this be so, it could never have been produced through the agency of natural selection alone.

We have further to ask.—How did man acquire his erect posture, his delicate yet expressive features, the marvellous beauty and symmetry of his whole external form;—a form which stands alone, in many respects more distinct from that of all the higher animals than they are from each other? Those who have lived much among savages know that even the lowest races of mankind, if healthy and well fed, exhibit the human form in its complete symmetry and perfection. They all have the soft smooth skin absolutely free from any hairy covering on the dorsal line, where all other mammalia from the Marsupials up to the Anthropoid apes have it most densely and strongly developed. What use can we conceive to have been derived from this exquisite beauty and symmetry and this smooth bare skin, both so very widely removed from his nearest allies? And if these modifications were of no physical use to him—or if, as appears almost certain in the case of the naked skin, they were at first a positive disadvantage—we know that they could not have been produced by natural selection. Yet we can well understand that

* See the admirable volume on the 'Hand,' by the late Sir Charles Bell, in the Bridgwater Treatise.

Geological Climates and the Origin of Species.   393

both these characters were essential to the proper development of the perfect human being. The supreme beauty of our form and countenance has probably been the source of all our æsthetic ideas and emotions, which could hardly have arisen had we retained the shape and features of an erect gorilla; and our naked skin, necessitating the use of clothing, has at once stimulated our intellect, and by developing the feeling of personal modesty may have profoundly affected our moral nature.

The same line of argument may be used in connexion with the structural and mental organs of human speech, since that faculty can hardly have been physically useful to the lowest class of savages; and if not, the delicate arrangements of nerves and muscles for its production could not have been developed and co-ordinated by natural selection. This view is supported by the fact that, among the lowest savages with the least copious vocabularies, the capacity of uttering a variety of distinct articulate sounds, and of applying to them an almost infinite amount of modulation and inflection, is not in any way inferior to that of the higher races. An instrument has been developed in advance of the needs of its possessor.

This subject is a vast one, and would require volumes for its proper elucidation, but enough, we think, has now been said, to indicate the possibility of a new stand-point for those who cannot accept the theory of evolution as expressing the whole truth in regard to the origin of man. While admitting to the full extent the agency of the same great laws of organic development in the origin of the human race as in the origin of all organized beings, there yet seems to be evidence of a Power which has guided the action of those laws in definite directions and for special ends. And so far from this view being out of harmony with the teachings of science, it has a striking analogy with what is now taking place in the world, and is thus strictly uniformitarian in character. Man himself guides and modifies nature for special ends. The laws of evolution alone would perhaps never have produced a grain so well adapted to his uses as wheat; such fruits as the seedless banana, and the bread-fruit; such animals as the Guernsey milch-cow, or the London dray-horse. Yet these so closely resemble the unaided productions of nature, that we may well imagine a being who had mastered the laws of development of organic forms through past ages, refusing to believe that any new power had been concerned in their production, and scornfully rejecting the theory that in these few cases a distinct intelligence had directed the action of the laws of variation, multiplication, and survival, for his own purposes. We know, however, that this

both

I think the same argument cd be applied to
any animal – what use of 5 toes to dogs foot

Plate 163. Charles Darwin's marginalia on his copy of Wallace's review of Charles Lyell's Principles of Geology, 10th edn, 2 vols, 1867–8, and Elements of Geology, 6th edn, 1865, published in Quarterly Review, 1869, vol.126, pp.359–94. Transcriptions of Darwin's pencilled notes by James Moore. From Darwin Archive 196.3, Cambridge University Library. (Reproduced by permission of the Syndics of Cambridge University Library.)

Plate 164.   Boeotian terracotta figurine of a young woman holding a mask in her right hand, dating probably from the early third century BCE, now in the British Museum, London, Inventory 1884.2–23.5 (from Tanagra?), 21.2 cm high. Art and artefacts provide important historical evidence about the conventions of staging in the ancient theatre.

Plate 166. Medea kills one of her sons. Campanian red-figure amphora, c.340–320 BCE, Ixion painter, Musée du Louvre, Paris. (Photograph: © AKG London/Erich Lessing.)

Plate 165. Medea demonstrates her rejuvenation technique on a ram in a boiling cauldron, watched by white-haired Pelias and his daughter. On the right a man stokes the fire underneath the cauldron. Attic black-figure Hydria from Vulci, c.510 BCE, British Museum, London, Inventory B328. (© British Museum, London.)

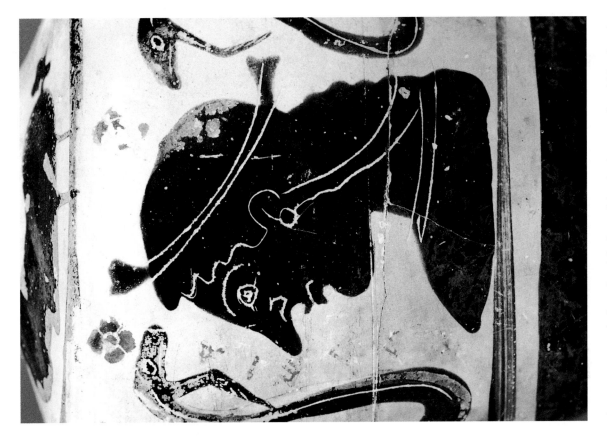

Plate 168. Head of Medea, lekythos of the Cock group, from Vulci, British Museum, London, Inventory 1926.4–17.1. (© The British Museum, London.)

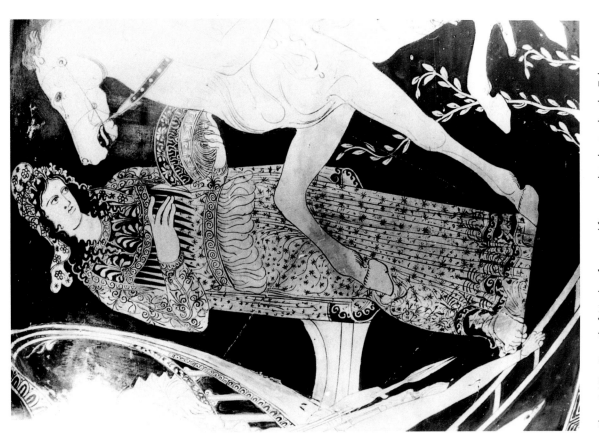

Plate 167. Detail of Medea from red-figure volute krater by the Talos painter, Museo Ruvo, Jatta 1501. (Reproduced by permission of Sir John Boardman, Athenian Red Figure Vases, The Classical Period, London, Thames and Hudson Ltd, 1989.)

Plate 169.   Medea and her children, detail from Apulian red-figure volute krater, c.330–310 BCE, attributed to the Underworld painter, Staatliche Antikensammlungen München, 3296. The whole vase is crowded with scenes from the story, including the death of the princess.

Plate 170.   Medea before the killing of her children, Roman wall painting from Pompeii, first century CE, Museo Nazionale, Naples.

Plate 171.   Medea and her children, Roman wall painting from Pompeii, first century CE, Museo Nazionale, Naples.

Plate 172. *Evelyn Pickering de Morgan, Medea, 1889, oil on canvas, 147 x 90 cm, Williamson Art Gallery and Museum, Birkenhead. The work was accompanied by a quotation 'Day by day/She saw the happy time fade fast away/And as she fell from out that happiness/Again she grew to be the Sorceress/Worker of fearful things, as she once was'. The setting resembles a temple with an altar to the left.*

Plate 173.   Valentine Cameron Prinsep, Medea the Sorceress, 1888, oil on canvas, 140 x 110 cm. South London Art Gallery. Medea is depicted collecting herbs and plants. A snake coiled round the tree perhaps brings with it the associations of Eve's fall in the Garden of Eden.

Plate 174. Frederick Sandys, Medea, completed 1868, oil on panel, 61 x 46 cm, Birmingham City Museum and Art Gallery. The work was rejected by the Royal Academy. The frieze in the background depicts Jason's ship and the Golden Fleece.

Plate 176. Li Lisha, who plays and talks about 'The Great Ambush' on AC11, with the p'i-p'a.
(Photograph: Mike Levers/The Open University.)

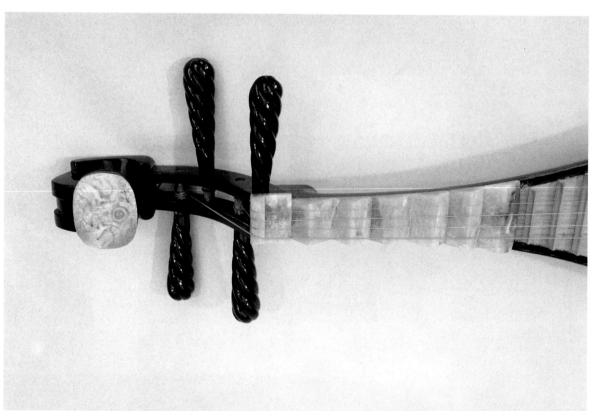

Plate 175. The neck of a modern Chinese p'i-p'a, showing the scroll, the tuning pegs and the jade frets.
(Photograph: Mike Levers/The Open University.)

Plate 177.   Andy Warhol, Jackie III, 1966, screenprint printed on white paper, 110 x 82.5 cm, Andy Warhol Foundation Inc./Art Resource, New York. (© 1998 The Andy Warhol Foundation for the Visual Arts/ARS, NY and DACS, London.)

Plate 178. Andy Warhol, White Burning Car II (White Disaster), 1963, acrylic and liquitex silkscreened on canvas, 269.5 x 209 cm, Museum für Moderne Kunst, Frankfurt. (Photograph: Robert Häusser. © 1998 ARS, NY and DACS, London.)

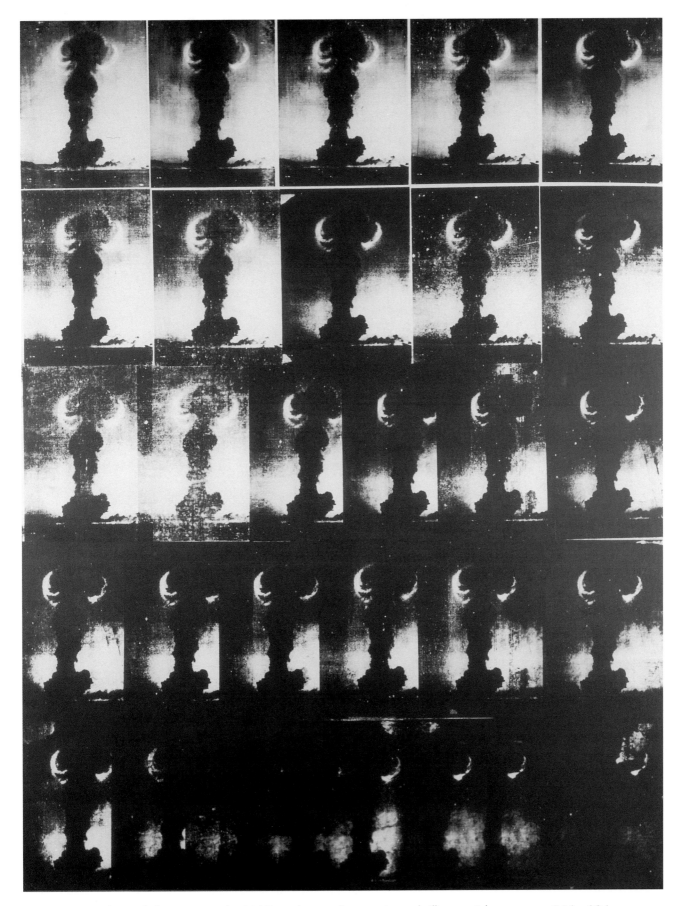

Plate 179.   Andy Warhol, Atomic Bomb, 1965, synthetic polymer paint and silkscreen ink on canvas, 264 x 204 cm,
Andy Warhol Foundation Inc./Art Resource, New York (© 1998 The Andy Warhol Foundation for the Visual Arts/ARS, NY.)

Plate 180. Pablo Picasso, The Charnel House, 1944–5, oil on canvas, 200 x 250 cm, Museum of Modern Art, New York. (© 1998 ARS, NY and DACS, London.)

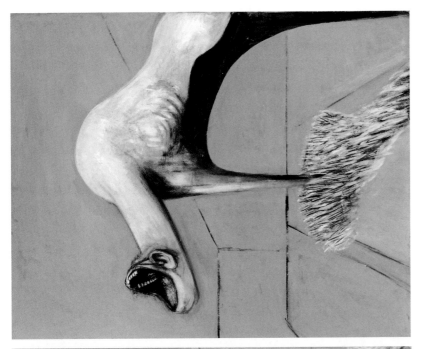

Plate 181.   Francis Bacon, Three Studies for Figures at the Base of a Crucifixion, c. 1944, oil on board, each panel 94 x 74 cm. (© The Tate Gallery, London.)

Plate 182. Mark Rothko, The Omen of the Eagle, 1942, oil and graphite on canvas, 65.5 x 45 cm, National Gallery of Art, Washington, D.C., gift of the Mark Rothko Foundation Inc. (© 1998 Board of Trustees, The National Gallery of Art, Washington, D.C. and ARS, NY and DACS, London.)

Plate 183. Andy Warhol, Eighty Two-Dollar Bills, Front and Rear, 1962, synthetic polymer paint and silkscreen on canvas, 211 x 96.5 cm, Museum Ludwig, Cologne. (© 1998 ARS, NY and DACS, London.)

Plate 184. Peter Paul Rubens, Susanna Lunden (Le Chapeau de Paille), c.1622, oil on wood, 79 x 54 cm, National Gallery, London. (Reproduced by courtesy of the Trustees, The National Gallery, London.)

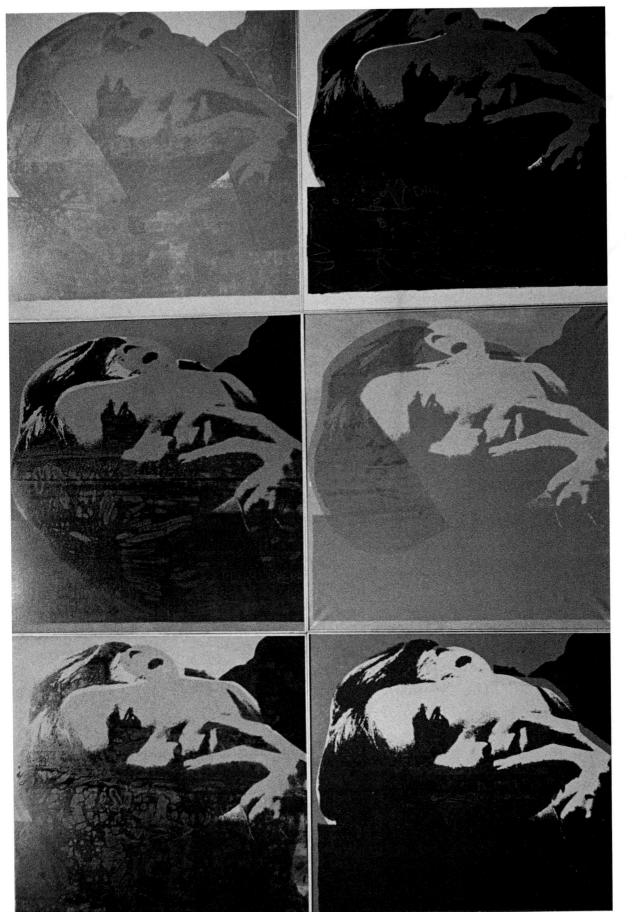

Plate 185. Andy Warhol, Self-portrait, 1967, acrylic and silkscreen enamel on canvas, each panel 180 x 180 cm, Leo Castelli, New York. (© 1998 ARS, NY and DACS, London.)

Plate 186.
George Morland, The Artist
in his Studio with his Man
Gibbs, c.1802, oil on
canvas, 76 x 64 cm,
Castle Museum Art Gallery,
Nottingham.

Printed in England by Spin Offset Ltd, Purfleet Industrial Park, Aveley, South Ockendon, Essex, RM15 4YA